COACHING
ZONE OFFENSE
BY THE EXPERTS

Edited by
Bob Murrey

COACHES CLINICS

ISBN: 1-58518-524-8

Library of Congress Catalog Card Number: 2001095165

Cover photo courtesy of Won-Up Productions

Cover design: Rebecca Gold

Text design: Jennifer Bokelmann

Coaches Choice
P.O. Box 1828
Monterey, CA 93942
http://www.coacheschoiceweb.com

Additional information on either the USA Coaches Clinic schedule or the USA Coaches library can be obtained by either calling 1-800-COACH-13 or faxing 1-314-991-1929.

> Throughout this book, the masculine shall be deemed to include the feminine and vice versa.

CONTENTS

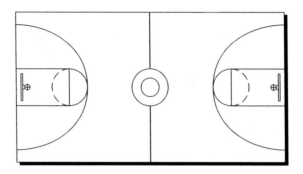

PLAYERS

(5) Centers

(3, 4) Forwards

(1, 2) Guards

◯ = Offense

X = Defense

⊙ = Player with the Ball

– – → = Direct Pass

——— = Screen

∿∿∿→ = Dribble

———→ = Cut of Player with or without the Ball

⊢⊢⊢⊢⊢⊢► = Shot

CHAPTER 1

ATTACKING ZONES

GENE BARTOW

I'd like to cover several points that I think are really important.

- If you can't convince your players that they must play hard, then they are going to lose.

- You must keep the turnovers down. Your players must be fundamentally sound. Have 8 or less per game and see what happens.

- You must be concerned about fouling. Keep those fouls down to 15 or less a game.

- Convince your players to be high percentage shooters. Don't let your players take bad shots. Get up around 50%.

- Convince your players of the importance of being high percentage free throw shooters.

- Find a way to communicate with the players and build confidence in those players. I've been lucky. I've had good players every year, even in high school. The one year that I spent at Illinois I had good players, but the problem there was that I was unable to convince them that they were good because they had lost so often the previous years. I knew they could win, but deep down they thought that something bad was going to happen in the last minute. But communicating a positive attitude to young people is extremely important. They will believe and play hard if you relate the right way.

It's also important that you keep on good terms with the people you work with, your fellow coaches, and your principal. In coaching, the controversial nature of the game keeps us moving from one place to another.

ATTACKING ZONES

No matter what type of zone offense that you use, you will need to address these seven points.

- *Patience.* You must convince your players to be patient.

- *Shot Selection.* Where do you shoot from and who shoots the ball?

- You must have *penetration* in the holes of the zone. Don't be content to pass the ball around the outside.

- *Overload.* Find ways of getting 4/3 and 3/2 situations. You must move men to accomplish this.

- *Screening.* Use skip-passes, and get ball into the block.
- *Offensive Rebounding.* This is very important. Work on this daily. When you play against a man defense, every man is checking out. But most zones have a difficult time of screening on the rebound.
- *Positive Thinking.* You must instill confidence. I believe that you must have a defensive philosophy centered around "me against you", man-to-man. I do use zones occasionally, but I am a man-to-man coach. Our team knows that, so when we see a zone, I tell my team that they don't think they can guard us or they wouldn't be in it.

I have a favorite zone offense, and we use it against any type of zone.

DIAGRAM 1-1.

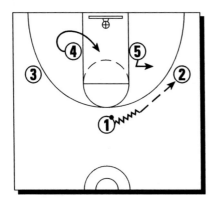

My best two shooters are 2 and 3, outside the 3-point line, post area extended. 4 and 5 are on the blocks. No matter which zone alignment it is, we are going to attack it with this 1-4 set. 1 passes to 2 to 5 or 1 to 2 to 4. Emphasize making that *extra pass* if you can't get it directly to the block.

DIAGRAM 1-2.

2 reverses back to 1, who takes two or three dribbles and passes to 3. Player 3 looks to 4. Player 5 screens on the other side. 3 can pass to 4 or else the skip-pass back to 2.

DIAGRAM 1-3.

It is hard to make the pass from the free throw line extended, but if he will make several dribbles toward the baseline, he can make the bounce pass inside.

DIAGRAM 1-4.

Any time the ball is reversed a second time, we will go into a high low situation.

DIAGRAM 1 5.

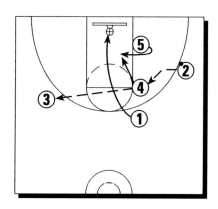

2 to 4 to 5, or 2 to 4 to 3, 1 crashes the board on the shot and either 2 or 3 is responsible for defensive balance.

DIAGRAM 1-6. ZONE #2, A STRAIGHT POWER ZONE.

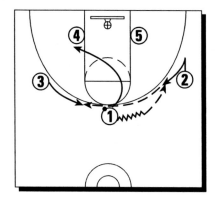

The set is similar except that the point guard will end up at the high post area. We really want to get the ball inside. 1 passes to 2 and exchanges with 3.

DIAGRAM 1-7.

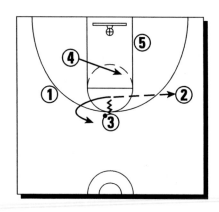

Remember, we are trying to get the ball inside. 3 goes to work, penetrates and passes to 2. Player 3 moves back to the point, 4 comes to the high post and we have a high-low situation.

DIAGRAM 1-8. 2 TO 4 TO 5

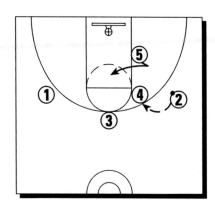

Don't underestimate getting the ball to the block from the corner area with the bounce pass.

DIAGRAM 1-9. ZONE #3

1 is the best shooter, often a guard. When we rotate out, we get outside the 3-point line. Why shoot a long two pointer? That's a horrible shot.

DIAGRAM 1-10.

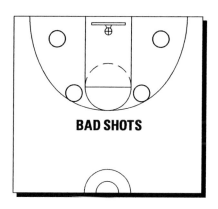

BAD SHOTS

I think these are bad shots.

DIAGRAM 1-11.

2 to 1 and he looks inside. If he cannot get the ball inside, 1 to 2 to 3 as 1 goes baseline off the screens of 5 and 4. He finds the holes in the zone and gets the ball back. He is your best shooter. 1 can then pass inside to 4.

DIAGRAM 1-12.

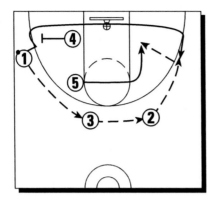

If nothing is open, 1 to 3 to 2 again. 1 can hit 5 coming down the lane. Have your good shooters shoot. *Don't let bad shooters shoot you out of the game.* I'm not interested in the star system. I'm interested in winning.

In attacking a 1-3-1 zone, we do things a little differently.

DIAGRAM 1-13.

We *fill the gaps* and try to get the ball to the block. Any time we get the ball to the baseline, we rotate someone to the ball.

DIAGRAM 1-14.

If the ball does not go inside, then as the ball comes out to the guard, the center returns to the other side of the lane. When attacking the 1-3-1, look for *the angle pass.* The ball goes from the forward to both guards and back to the forward. We also look for the lob near the basket.

DIAGRAM 1-15.

Fill the gaps, 2 to 3, but not able to get the ball inside. Return to 2, to 1 who is the point guard. 1 penetrates the gap and 4 drops down. 1 can pass to 4 to 5 or to 3. Make the extra pass against the zone. Emphasize the extra pass.

CHAPTER 2

ZONE OFFENSE

JOHN CALIPARI

We run 4 motion around our center. It is simple but it gets us to attack the basket. We used to go 3 out and 2 in and I was giving the kids too much credit, as if they knew how to attack the zone. We got nothing. So, we came up with this simple offense with some rotation. This is good against a matchup zone. We want to move people, cutting and moving hurts a matchup zone. We also want to move the ball, then knife the zone. The more you move the ball, the more confused the matchup gets. We wanted to penetrate by the use of the dribble and/ or the pass.

DIAGRAM 2-1.

This is structured motion. I think that a match-up is hurt by this. When the ball is passed, the passer cuts and then that spot is filled by another player.

DIAGRAM 2-2.

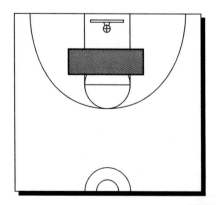

I always want one man in this area against a match-up.

DIAGRAM 2-3.

This is the setup. In fact this is the way we start against either man or zone.

DIAGRAM 2-4.

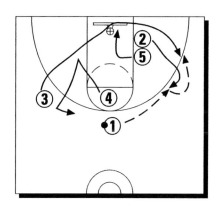

1 passes to 2 and 3 cuts to the grey area, or dead area, whatever you call it. 4 cuts to the basket and then out. If 2 passes to 3, 3 looks to 5. If 2 passes directly to 5, he stays.

DIAGRAM 2-5.

If 2 swings the ball, he cuts and hesitates for one or two seconds in the middle. If we can pass to 2 there, we do. 5 is moving to the weakside rebounding position. If 1 doesn't pass to 2, he passes to 4.

DIAGRAM 2-6.

4 can pass to 2 in the grey area who would look to 5. If 4 reverses the ball he cuts with the one or two second hesitation in the middle. 5 chases, and 2 then fills in behind. 4 can also skip pass to 3.

DIAGRAM 2-7.

My players are all similar. That's why we run this. If 2 shoots the ball, 5 rolls to the middle to rebound. 4 races to the offside board. 3 goes to the board. 1 and 2 are back. 4 and 5 always rebound, 3 goes sometimes, depending on his position.

DIAGRAM 2-8.

This is what makes this effective. 1 dribbles to the wing. 2 starts up and then to the corner. 2 goes through when 1 passes to 4. Player 4 passes to 3. Then 2 cuts hard baseline, 5 follows hard, and 4 cuts to the basket. We get good shots just from this setup and by working the ball.

DIAGRAM 2-9.

Now you are in this. 3 can now make a skip-pass to 4. 5 will chase across, 3 will fill in behind him or else precede 5 and go to the corner. Notice that two men don't move. 1 stays at the top of the key, looking for penetration if the zone spreads. 5 goes from block to block, chasing the ball.

DIAGRAM 2-10. TOP CUT

3 has the ball, 4 is low. 3 passes to 1 to 2 to 4. Player 3 starts to cut and comes back. 4 just continued on to the basket. This zone offense gave us structure with motion. It's hard to play a match-up zone against motion. If you have a good 5 man, he is always around the ball and can score. If he can't play, he becomes a passer. Now we use him as he cuts as a passer.

DIAGRAM 2-11.

He can pass out to the weakside for the three-point shot. If he doesn't have a layup, he is a passer. If 3 passes to 5, 4 ducks in. 5 always stays above the block.

DIAGRAM 2-12.

1 passes to 4 who can pass to 3. Or 1 can pass directly to 5, who can pass to 3. The whole idea is we are moving bodies, moving the ball and then we look to knife the zone, either on the dribble, the jump stop in the lane, or a pass.

DIAGRAM 2-13.

Here is a dribble entry. 1 dribbles at 2 who goes to the corner. 1 looks to 5. Player 4 steps out for the reversal. 1 passes to 4 who passes to 3. On that pass to 4, 2 cuts hard into the grey area. Or he can cut all the way through. 5 can come across or stay depending on the defense. If 5 thinks he can get the post position, he will come across. If not, he'll bump and come right back. On the reversal, 3 goes through, 4 goes to the basket, 1 comes back. If they cover 2 and 5, we are looking for 4. No matter which offense you are running, try getting into it with this action.

DIAGRAM 2-14.

As 4 leaves, 1 fills in. When the ball is reversed again, from 3 to 1 to 4, 2 and 5 again cut across.

DIAGRAM 2-15. DRILL

This is with a coach and 3 players. This is without 5, who works on duck-ins and flash cuts. For these 3 players, coach passes to 2. If 2 passes to 3, everyone stays. If 2 passes to coach, 2 cuts looking for the ball. Coach passes to 4.

DIAGRAM 2-16.

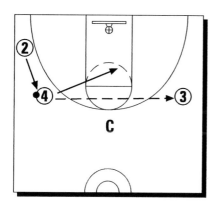

If 4 passes to 2, everyone stays. If 4 skip-passes to 3, 4 chases the pass and 2 fills in. These 3 players are working on that action to get to know each other. If you cut, you are in good shape. And someone must fill in behind. I want to emphasize the philosophy and the concepts that we use, attacking the basket and keeping the ball below shoulder level. Even attacking the zone, we do not put the ball over the head. I want them in the attack mode. We are trying to get them to play harder than their opponent and to do that we must keep it simple.

Question—Will this work against any type of zone?

Answer—It is best against a match-up, but it will work versus a 2-3. The 1-2-2 gives you a little trouble because they have 4 players out also. What we run against a 1-2-2 is a baseline runner with two players on the block. We overload on the baseline. I believe that you must move the ball, move the men, and get the ball in the lane. I ask the kids, "Why are they playing zone?" They are playing zone to protect themselves in the lane. They don't want us to go in there, so that's where we want to go. So, we don't rely on plays as much as we rely on players knowing how to play. We have a coaches' mailing at our school. We send things out to coaches. If you want to be a part of that mailing send me your address. It's a great way to communicate with coaches all over the country. Just address it to me at the Basketball Office at the University of Massachusetts and say you'd like to be a part of the coaches' mailing.

CHAPTER 3

ZONE OFFENSE

EDDIE FOGLER

T-GAME—DIAGRAMS 3-1 TO 3-15

DIAGRAM 3-1.

These spots are filled when the ball is in the corner.

DIAGRAM 3-2.

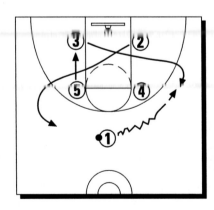

Continuity begins with the ball reversing.

DIAGRAM 3-3.

With the ball moving to the other side, 3, 4, and 5 shift.

DIAGRAM 3-4.

Diagrams 3-4 to 3-6 show the movements when the ball is reversed again.

DIAGRAM 3-5.

DIAGRAM 3-6.

DIAGRAM 3-7.

Diagram 3-7 shows a box set from which you can start. 1 picks a side.

DIAGRAM 3-8.

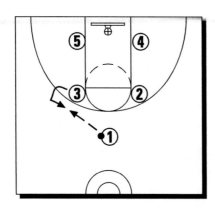

1 can also pass to 3.

DIAGRAM 3-9.

We want 2 to go out and the opposite post to go low.

SCORING OPTIONS:

DIAGRAM 3-10.

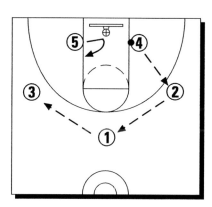

5 cuts to the basket if 4 receives the ball at the low post, not looking to score until the ball goes to the opposite side.

DIAGRAM 3-11.

On the pass to the high post, his first look is low to 4 crossing the lane, then to 2 on the weakside.

DIAGRAM 3-12.

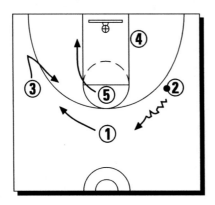

2 can release with the dribble. If it breaks down, just fill the spots.

DIAGRAM 3-13.

2 can go back to 5 at the high post, who can go weakside again.

DIAGRAM 3-14."PINCH"

2 dribbles off the high post for a screen and roll.

DIAGRAM 3-15. LOB PLAY

3 blocks the man in middle; 5 blocks the man in back; 4 cuts to the basket.

CHAPTER 4

ATTACKING THE MATCH-UP ZONE

PETE GILLEN

My goal is to give each and every one of you something that will make your team a little better next year; a drill, a thought, a concept. At Xavier, we have a 10-minute meeting before practice. It sets the tone. We talk about basketball, but we also talk about life. We put examples on the bulletin board about things to do and things not to do. One of our biggest problems is getting our players to do what is right. We want them to keep on the straight and narrow.

My topic today is *"attacking the match-up zone."*

Just what is a match-up? There are a lot of ways to play a match-up, many different types. The following is a brief idea of what it is:

DIAGRAM 4-1.

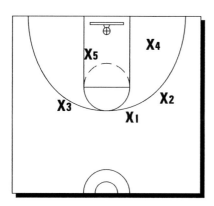

A match-up is a zone *with man-to-man principles.* In a match-up, the man is just as important as the ball. Each defensive player has a man in his area and he is just as important as the ball. The zone will have different alignments depending on the offense. Whatever the offense is in, the defense is in the same set. X1 is usually your point guard. The rest of the players key off of him. The first man to his left is X2 and he takes the first player to X1's left. If there is no one there, he drops all the way to the baseline to find him. X3 has the first man to X1's right. X5 has the post man, wherever he is. X4 is the *"rover."* He has the second man from X1.

DIAGRAM 4-2.

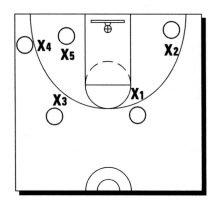

If the offense is in a 2-3 alignment, then the defense adjusts.

DIAGRAM 4-3.

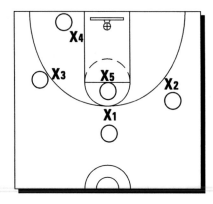

If the offense is a 1-3-1, then the zone is a 1-3-1. Again, the rover is two men over.

DIAGRAM 4-4.

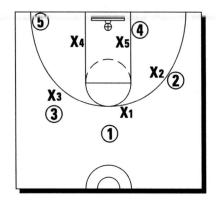

If you are in a 1-2-2, X5 takes the center, and X4 takes the second man. Some match-ups will actually go through with the cutter on one side. But usually, when the ball is passed, the men will switch players.

How do we attack the match-up? It is 80% mental. The purpose of the match-up zone is to get you confused, indecisive; to get you out of sync.

We are going to *act*, and *not react*. We tell them, don't worry about it. We are going to run the offense that we want to run.

We want to attack with the fast break, which is the toughest thing to defend in basketball. Send four players to the offensive boards. One of the toughest things to teach in the match-up is screening out on the rebounds. We want to be aggressive.

DIAGRAM 4-5. DRIBBLE PENETRATION

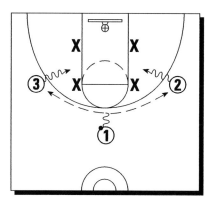

Don Casey is a great teacher of the zone. I asked him what hurts the zone the most. His reply was *dribble penetration*. We *attack the zone with the dribble*.

DIAGRAM 4-6.

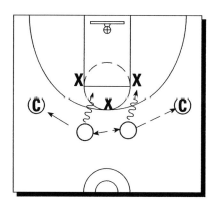

Then, we attack the odd-front zone with two guards and two coaches vs. three defensive men. You must work at dribble penetration.

Screen the zone in different areas. Screen at the point, at the wing, in the corners, and in the low-post area. We want to cause confusion and indecision for the defense. We want to change the offensive look periodically. Don't stay in the same offense. Don't get stereotyped.

OUR 10 PRINCIPLES VS. THE MATCH-UP

Send cutters through. Cutters cause indecision. Who's got him? There is a *moment of confusion.* If you just stand, you are doing the match-up a favor. *Attack the baseline* and reverse the ball to the other baseline.

DIAGRAM 4-7.

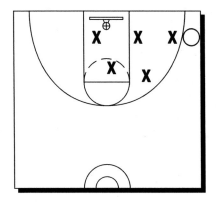

Many zones are high, especially with the 3-point shot. There is room on the baseline. When you get the ball on the baseline all the zones are the same; they are all like a 2-3 zone. Someone must cover the wing, someone must be in the low post, someone must slide down and help and the weakside sags. If they *trap in the corner,* we don't send the ball there immediately.

DIAGRAM 4-8.

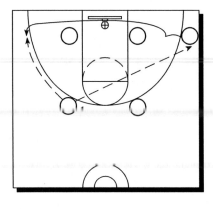

We fake to the corner, pass to the other guard and then either bring him across on the baseline or make the *skip-pass* to him.

Dribble Penetration. You want to drive, but you want to *drive after several passes*. You *must stretch the zone first*. We have a rule:

DIAGRAM 4-9.

Anytime we get the ball from the wing, no matter what type of zone, *the point man must go as deep as he can*. Penetrate under control and look to pass to the wing or the post.

DIAGRAM 4-10. COME FROM BEHIND THE ZONE

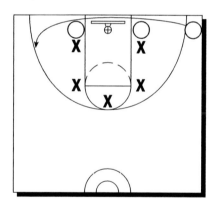

Coming from behind causes indecision. We want cutters coming, but men ducking in.

DIAGRAM 4-11. SCREEN THE ZONE

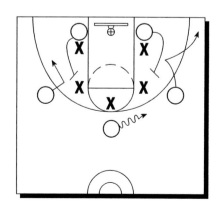

Screen the wings. The point guard must dribble at the wing, our wings fade to the corner. This puts pressure on the back man. Does he stay in or play the man in the corner?

DIAGRAM 4-12.

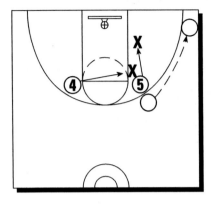

If we make the pass to the corner, 5 rolls to the basket and 4 fills the high post, so we have a quick 2-on-1 on the back of the zone with the corner and 5.

DIAGRAM 4-13.

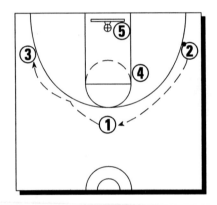

If the corner passes back to the point, the ball is reversed to 3. All of this comes from screening the wing.

DIAGRAM 4-14.

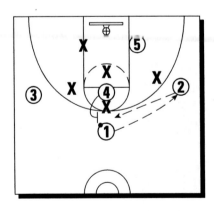

We also screen the point. 1 passes to 2, 4 screens the point. The ball is passed back to the point.

DIAGRAM 4-15.

We have a screen and roll with 4 and 1. 3 fades to the baseline. 1 can take the jumper, dribble into the gut of the zone and pass to 3 if X3 comes up to stop the drive.

DIAGRAM 4-16.

He can pass to 5. If we pass to 3 in the corner, X5 must cover him, so 5 comes across the lane. X3 is coming to 3. X5 must either play 5 or 4 because of his high/low situation.

DIAGRAM 4-17.

We also like to *screen in the block area*. They are matched up, but when the ball is reversed, 4 screens the back of the zone. Then 4 ducks in. Don't flash to the ball unless you screen first.

DIAGRAM 4-18.

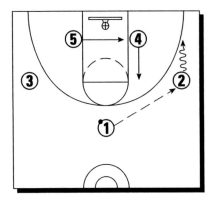

Have the wing dribble to the corner. Who takes him? 4 comes up the lane. 5 comes behind.

DIAGRAM 4-19.

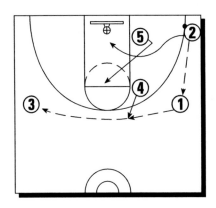

Now we have a *box overload*. We back-pick with 5 as we step out with 4 and reverse the ball. We send 2 across, but we are already looking for 5 ducking in after the screen. Ball goes 2-1-3-2-5.

SKIP-PASS AFTER A BALL FAKE.

Stretch out the zone. You can't telegraph it, you must freeze the zone. Send four men to the offensive boards.

DIAGRAM 4-20. DUCK-IN AND SEAL BACK MOVE

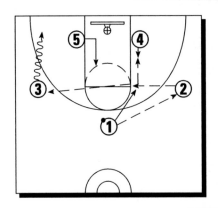

1 to 2, back to 1. Player 5 ducks in and 1 looks to get 5 the ball. Notice 5 moves the defense by moving several steps along the baseline before ducking in. If 1 can't pass to 5, pass to 3. 3 dribbles hard to the baseline and 5 returns to his original spot to receive a bounce pass from 3. The ball goes 1-2-1-3-5.

DIAGRAM 4-21. WING TO POINT TO POST

1 passes to 2, back to 1, and 4 comes up the lane. Also, 5 can duck in for the pass from 1. It is difficult to defend because the post is being fronted when the ball is on the wing.

DIAGRAM 4-22.

You must have the *3-point shot vs. the match-up.* We have an *attack set.* 2 pops out, 1 passes to 2, and goes off the post. The low man in the zone will take the cutter. The *wing will be covered.*

DIAGRAM 4-23.

We are going to *screen the wing.* 5 back-screens, 2 goes on the dribble and runs the pick-and-roll toward the center of the floor. The match-up will switch. 5 will now set another screen on the back side. As soon as 2 comes off the screen, 4 screens the other back players on the zone and 3 pops out for the 3-point shot. 4 *then ducks in.*

DIAGRAM 4-24.

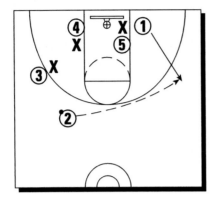

We have a double down-screen. 2 can pass to 1 for the 3-point attempt. He passes back against the grain. The *first option is the 3-point shot by 1.*

DIAGRAM 4-25.

1 can dribble to the baseline and bounce pass inside to 5.

Let's talk about the whole offense vs. the match-up. The biggest thing is not to worry about what you are doing. Do what you want to do, and *be positive with your kids.* This is more important than the X and O stuff.

DIAGRAM 4-26.

This is a 1-2-2 match-up. 4 and 5 are on the blocks. We can go either side. We like to *bump against a match-up.* By "bump," we mean that we start in one direction behind the defense, then reverse and stay on the same side. This causes problems. 3 bumps to the corner. It is important that 1 dribbles at the wing. Remember our theory. *Get the ball to one baseline and attack the defense from the other.*

DIAGRAM 4-27.

4 screens the block area. 3 runs the baseline; 4 screens and looks for the duck-in. 5 screens and then ducks in. Reverse the ball to the other baseline. *4 has the option of going to the elbow.*

DIAGRAM 4-28.

If 4 doesn't get the ball, he goes back to the block. 3 makes the skip-pass to 1 and runs the baseline. 5 screens and ducks in.

DIAGRAM 4-29.

Another possibility is for 3 to cut into the middle of the zone as 1 drives at the wing. 3 then slides out to the corner. 1 can pass to 3 or 5, depending on what X5 does.

DIAGRAM 4-30.

If X5 goes to the corner, we bounce pass to 5 on the block or to 4 coming to the elbow.

DIAGRAM 4-31. THE DRIBBLE IN MOVE

1 dribbles at 2 and 2 goes to the foul line area. Who's going to play him from their 1-2-2 set? 1 can pass to 2.

DIAGRAM 4-32.

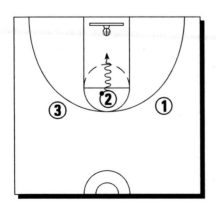

If 1 doesn't pass to 2, 2 goes down and opposite.

DIAGRAM 4-33.

If 1 passes to 3, 2 goes to the opposite corner. *4 screens the back of the zone.* 3 can skip-pass to 2; 5 flashes to the elbow. The ball can go 1-3-2-3 or 1-3-2-5.

DIAGRAM 4-34.

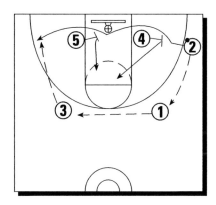

If nothing happens, 2 reverses the ball to 1 to 3, and 2 runs the baseline with *4 and 5 screening and ducking into the middle.*

DIAGRAM 4-35. STACK SET

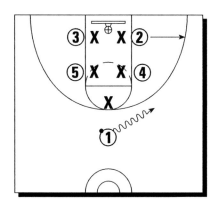

The stack presents a match-up problem. 1 dribbles and 2 pops to the corner. This is our man offense. Don't do the same thing time after time against the match-up. *3 comes out high.*

DIAGRAM 4-36.

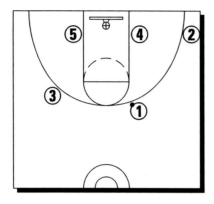

So now we are set as illustrated in Diagram 4-36. This is basically the same formation, but you are disguising it with your double stack.

DIAGRAM 4-37. MOTION FROM THE STACK

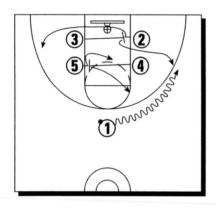

The more cutters, the more confusion we get. 1 dribbles to the right, 3 screens to 2 and 2 goes to the corner. 3 goes to the corner. On the pass from 1 to 3, we have a screen away. 5 goes low. 4 comes high after the screen. 5 will usually be covered, but 4 will be open.

DIAGRAM 4-38.

After the cuts, 1 cuts down the middle of the lane and goes away. Sometimes 1 replaces himself.

DIAGRAM 4-39.

Here is a *set play* that will spread the zone. 2 pops out, 1 passes to 2. This is the old UCLA shuffle cut off the stack. 1 cuts down the middle.

DIAGRAM 4-40.

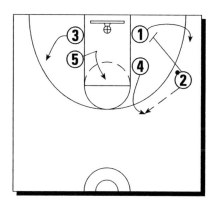

2 passes to 4 who moves high and 2 then screens down for 1. *5 ducks in and 3 pops out.* The ball goes from 1-2-3-1 or 1-2-4-3-5. We ran the zone offense with the cutters, the slides, the dribble in, the motion, and we ran the UCLA shuffle cut. You give them a lot of *different looks.*

DIAGRAM 4-41.

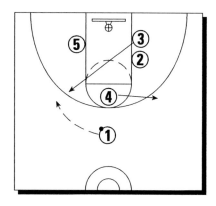

We like to bring the ball to one side and attack the other side. Stacks give them trouble. 1 takes the ball to the left. 4 goes away. 3 comes to the top of the key area.

DIAGRAM 4-42.

5 acts as if he is screening, and then pivots and seals. 1 passes to 5 or back to 3. 5 comes up the lane. When the ball is passed from the wing to the point, 4 screens the bottom of the zone for 2. 3 can pass back to 1 back to 5. 3 can pass directly to 5. 3 can pass to 2 and inside to 4. 3 can pass directly to 4.

DIAGRAM 4-43.

If 3 dribbles across ,we have the triangle, and 3 can pass to 1 to 5 or 3 can pass to 2 to 4.

Remember, against the match-up, run what you want to run and take the ball at the defense.

CHAPTER 5

ATTACKING ZONES

CRAIG HARTMAN

In theory, the best way to beat a zone is to *beat it down the floor* and not allow it to set up. In a man-to-man defense, the defense might say who will play whom, but on offense I can determine where you'll play my man. In a zone the defense says who will play where on defense and on offense; I'll say who you'll play against. An example would be if you had a slow forward on the left side of the zone, we would put one of our quicker players on the baseline against him.

DIAGRAM 5-1.

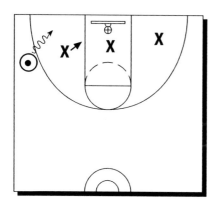

Our major concept of beating a zone is to *distort* a zone. The best way to do this is to *dribble* against it.

We also want our players to get into the *gaps* of a zone; see Diagrams 5-2 and 5-3.

DIAGRAM 5-2.

DIAGRAM 5-3.

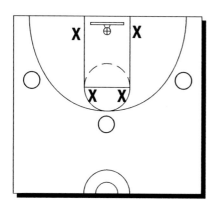

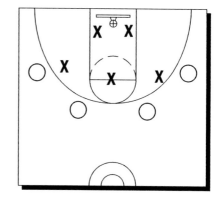

DIAGRAM 5-4.

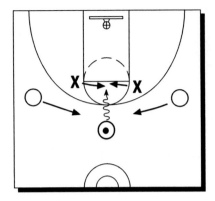

We will use the dribble to take the ball into the *gaps* of the zone.

DIAGRAM 5-5.

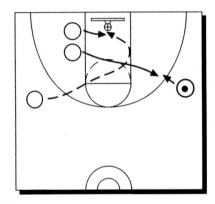

"Freeze" a defensive player.

DIAGRAM 5-6.

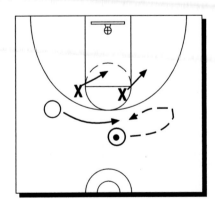

Move the zone one way so we can *pass opposite*.

DIAGRAM 5-7.

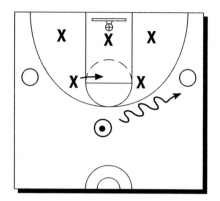

We can take all these concepts and combine them into one movement.

DIAGRAM 5-8.

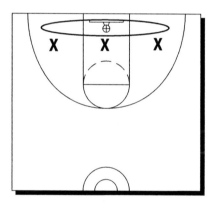

We also want to attack the zone from *behind*. We like to start players low, behind the *bottom line* of the zone. This will *force* the zone to drop lower and *open up* the middle more. If the zone doesn't drop to cover these low-post players, this opens up the opportunity for a *lob pass* low and an easy basket.

DIAGRAM 5-9.

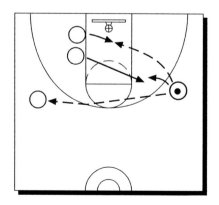

If we *flash* a man into the high post and make the pass inside to him, his rules are to catch the ball, look to shoot, look low for a layup, or look to the opposite wing.

DIAGRAM 5-10.

When our guards bring the ball down the sideline on the break or off the offense, we want them to take the ball *below* the foul line extended before we look to pass because this move will force the zone to *move and extend* itself, thus opening up some passing lanes.

We use different alignments to attack a zone. Our players set up in the *gaps* of the zone to start the offense. Some alignments we have used are as follows:

DIAGRAM 5-11. TRIPLE LOW

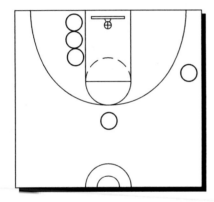

DIAGRAM 5-12. DOUBLE LOW

DIAGRAM 5-13. HIGH LOW

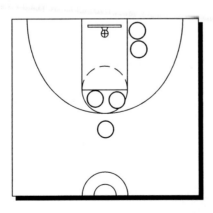

DIAGRAM 5-14.
DOUBLE LOW, SINGLE HIGH

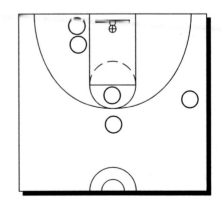

DIAGRAM 5-15. TRIPLE HIGH, SINGLE LOW

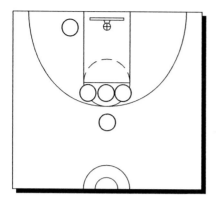

Remember, you want to start in an alignment that will put the zone defense at a *disadvantage.* We also use what we call a *dribble clear* to create an *advantage* against the zone. We can do this from the top or side of the zone.

DIAGRAM 5-16.

From the top, the point would dribble the ball to the wing area. Upon seeing this dribble move, the wing player would make what we call a *shallow cut* into the center of the zone and then out to the top of the key.

DIAGRAM 5-17.

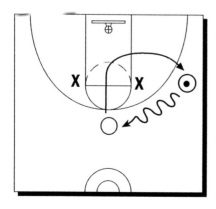

When he cuts into the middle, the wing will delay a second to see if he might be open for a pass inside. If the ball is *dribble-cleared* from the wing to the point, the point man would make a shallow cut into the center of the zone and out to the vacated wing position.

DIAGRAM 5-18.

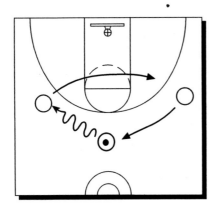

On a *dribble-clear* to the wing, we can also have the wing cut completely through the zone to the *opposite wing* and have the wing on weakside fill the point position.

DIAGRAM 5-19.

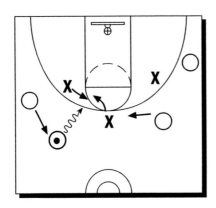

In attacking an *odd-front zone* 1-2-2, 1-3-1, 3-2, you want to determine the *movement* of the top/middle players. The more they extend the zone out, the more you want to attack this move. We tell our guards to start the ball wide and *attack the gaps* of the top with a *hard dribble.*

You must also stress *footwork* In attacking the zone. All potential shooters must be in shooting position when they receive the ball. They must have their off-foot up, strong foot back, and shoulders square to the basket so that when they receive the pass, they can step directly into their shot. There was no one better than Steve Alford in doing this.

Emphasize *pass fakes and shot fakes* versus the zone. The zone is taught to react to the ball, so we feel these two fakes will open up passing lanes if they are executed properly.

What do we do versus a *box and one?* We will take the man being guarded man-to-man and use him as a *screener.* We place him in the middle of the box and tell him to *screen.*

DIAGRAM 5-20.

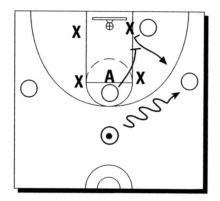

For example, A is being played man-to-man, so we would place him at the high post, have the point guard dribble at one of the top players to *"freeze"*him, and have A slide down and screen the bottom forward.

This move would open the wing for a *clear shot.* If the guard doesn't respect the point's *"freeze"* dribble, he can turn into the lane and shoot the jumper.

DIAGRAM 5-21.

We can also screen the low post for a move to the corner for a jumper.

CHAPTER 6

ZONE OFFENSE

JOHN KRESSE

In earlier years, the zone defense was designed to allow teams to place larger line-ups on the floor, force opponents to score from the perimeter and dominate rebounding statistics. However, zone defenses seemed to become obsolete with the emergence of the three-point shot that forced defenses to step out and guard players man-to-man. But, being the creative lot that we are, coaches have again discovered how to play good zone defense while protecting against long-range bombs. Therefore, it has again become strategically important to design an offensive system to that will be successful against zone defenses.

It is often thought that the most successful offense against a zone defense is a reliable and effective fast break. However, most successful teams must also possess solid perimeter shooting, effective penetration, a strong inside game and sound rebounding in order to beat a zone defense. It is our theory that an "inside - out" approach will yield great dividends against a zone. By this, we mean that we would like to establish our inside players as our *primary offensive options* so as to force the zone to focus on them, then leaving our perimeter players open to shoot and drive. This tactic will often provide many high percentage shots, draw countless fouls, allow shooters to spot-up for shots and keep big players happy.

From an offensive standpoint, we believe the most crucial point of each possession is how quickly our players *recognize* a zone defense and *adjust* to it. Poise and patience in this situation are paramount In order to get a high percentage shot. Spacing is stressed in every offensive set, preferably fifteen feet between players as this will allow for cuts and ball reversal. Above all, timing must be perfect to allow passes to be delivered when the cutter is in the best scoring position. Further, we believe that we can create mismatches against zones by creating offensive triangles with our players that often yield 3-on-2 or even 2-on-1 situations.

In each offensive series that we run against zones, we look to include the use of cutters, ball fakes, ball reversal and lobs behind the zone in order to force our opponent to *adjust* defensively. Years ago, players were taught to simply whip the ball around the zone, wearing the defense out until a good shot could be had. However, with the increase in athletic ability of players at every level, it now becomes important to use these suggested tactics for success. It now is even more critical that players receive the ball in a fundamental triple threat position and step into all shots. We recommend that players be taught to pass the ball to targets *away from the defense* in dummy situations on the practice floor. The final result for any program is the achievement of a good, high percentage shot that is within a player's range or that is the result of a good individual move that frees him to finish the play or get fouled.

Zones often provide *gaps* that, when exploited by cutters or penetration, will often yield productive offensive situations. If a player beats the defense through a gap, he has beaten two-fifths of the defense to the basket. Therefore, we ask our point guards to be conscious of this possibility and always utilize a *reverse dribble* for the purpose of possibly exploding through a gap or creating a passing lane to get us into our offense.

Against zones, we look to employ both set plays and continuities that will provide organization, player and ball movement and rebounding. Diagrams 6-1 through 6-6 illustrate two of our favorite set plays (i.e., Carolina and Red Series). In running a continuity, players operate patterned movements, as well as ball movement, to gain an open shot. These series may take as many as eight passes to be successful. On the other hand, set plays are quick hitting tactics that create scoring opportunities for a team's most gifted players. It is a coach's responsibility to tell players how to attack the opponent, show them how to carry out the strategy and then make sure that they execute the game plan. If a staff accomplishes these goals, as well as insists on sound defense and good shot selection, success will be inevitable regardless of the defense.

DIAGRAM 6-1.

DIAGRAM 6-2.

DIAGRAM 6-3.

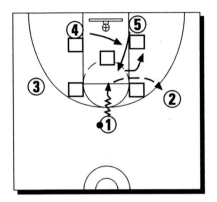

DIAGRAM 6-4.

DIAGRAM 6-5.

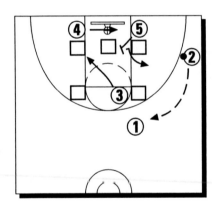

DIAGRAM 6-6.

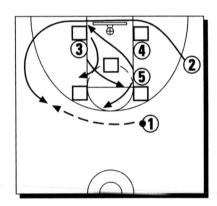

CHAPTER 7

ATTACKING ZONE DEFENSES

ANDY LANDERS

We get a lot of offense from our defense. In your eyes it might not be organized, but in our eyes it is organized because that is what we practice every day. If you have a good shot when you get to the other end, shoot it. If not, back it out. As you back it out, look for the secondary break. If it is not there, usually we will run motion.

DIAGRAM 7-1.

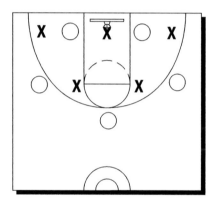

I want to give you my thoughts about zone offenses rather than giving you a zone offense. We set up the opposite of how the defense sets up. If you are in a 2-guard front, we are in a point-guard set.

DIAGRAM 7-2.

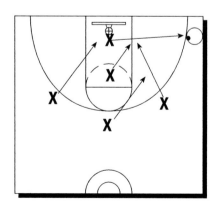

When the ball is in the corner, all zone defenses are 2-3. It doesn't matter how they start. It seems to me that is something to attack; something good to know.

DIAGRAM 7-3.

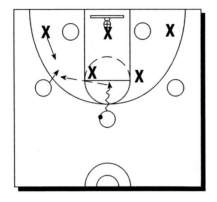

We must attack gaps and the baseline. Do you teach driving into the gap and drawing two defenders and then kick out to the wing? This makes the back man come up and leave the baseline open. Can you manipulate the zone? Can you make certain people go to certain spots and defend like you want them to do? If you can do that, then you can attack however you want.

DIAGRAM 7-4.

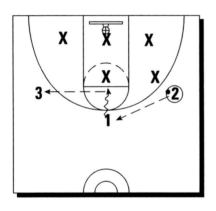

The point guard, 1, passes to the wing, 2, and the defensive guard moves over to guard him. The ball is passed back to 1, and 1 does not attack the gap. 1 attacks X1. X1 must defend 1, who then passes to 3 and makes the back man come out to guard him. Does he have to shoot every time? No. But if he never shoots, the zone will not come out to guard him. You will play the player who is weak defensively if she can score. You will devise an offense for her. If you don't have shooters, start a program to develop them. High school coaches don't have enough time to make shooters out of players. They must be taught before you get them.

DIAGRAM 7-5.

Anytime the offside post, 4, sees the baseline man going out to defend the wing, that is an automatic short corner cut.

DIAGRAM 7-6.

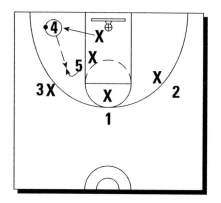

If the baseline player goes out to guard the short corner, then we pass low-high, 4 to 5. We want 5 to step up the lane away from the ball.

DIAGRAM 7-7.

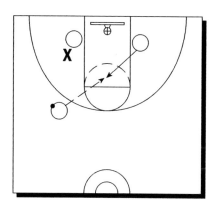

Teach you post players to read the defense. If the ball is on the wing, the post player can make an automatic flash.

DIAGRAM 7-8.

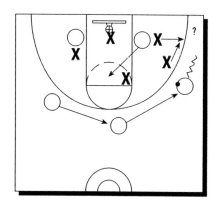

Do your guards know this? Do they know that they can use a wag dribble to distort the defense? How far will the defense go with the guard? Will she go all the way to the corner? Or will the back player step out and play her? Anytime our guard wags down, the top guard rotates over and the wing rotates up.

DIAGRAM 7-9.

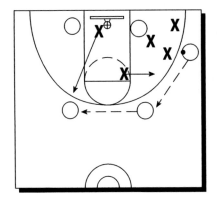

Reverse the ball to the wing and you know that the back defender doesn't want to come high, but they will. If they don't, we shoot it. If they do, we pass in to the post.

DIAGRAM 7-10.

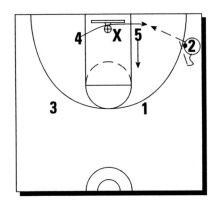

You can also wag dribble out of the corner. How far will the back man come? The weakside post, 4, goes to the short corner and 5 moves up the lane as the ball is passed to the short corner.

DIAGRAM 7-11.

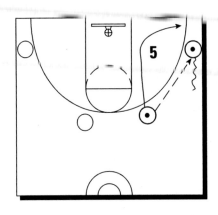

We don't have a lot of schemes against a zone, we have reads. We can also use the wag dribble out of the corner and if we are in a four out set, we can send a perimeter player to the short corner. Anytime the ball is passed to the corner, we cut through. But if the ball is dribbled, we come back to the short corner.

DIAGRAM 7-12.

Anytime that the ball drives baseline, the weakside wing goes to the baseline for the skip-pass.

DIAGRAM 7-13.

Let's put it all together. 1 dribbles into the gap and passes to 2. X5 comes out to guard 2. 4 automatically breaks to the short corner. If the ball is passed to the short corner, 5 moves up the lane.

DIAGRAM 7-14.

If the ball is not shot from the short corner and cannot be passed directly to 5, the ball is passed to 1 and then back to 5, who has sealed.

DIAGRAM 7-15.

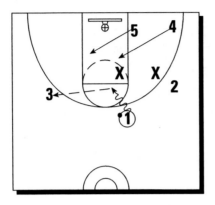

If the ball is not passed directly to 5, 1 attacks the guard and then passes to 3 on the weakside. 5 steps in and 4 follows.

CHAPTER 8

OFFENSIVE THEORIES AGAINST A ZONE

Rick Majerus

FIVE THINGS TO CONSIDER:

- Alignment
- Plays
- Basics
- Sequences
- Principles

SIX BASICS FOR PERIMETER PLAYERS:

- Quick pass—never look to pass into the post on the first pass.
- Shot—must have a readiness to shoot with hand targets.
  No shot on the first side.
- Shot fake—teach 6" step and a 6" lift with the ball.
  Use a permanent pivot foot. Allow no re-cock of the ball after a fake; produce an economy of motion.
- Pass fake—post flashes on a pass fake; this sets up counter-flow action.
- Gap dribble
- Lateral dribble

FOUR BASICS FOR POST PLAYERS:

All post players must be able to identify your go-to move and your go-to side. The coach must know which block he operates from best.

- Post
- Backscreen and post
- Flash—and flash hard. Don't move while the ball is in the air; wait until the reception.
- Step out or step up. Step out to the short corner or up the lane to create a passing lane. (Diagram 8-1)

DIAGRAM 8-1. STEP OUT OR STEP UP

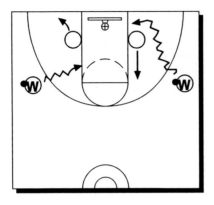

MOVEMENTS VS. A ZONE

- Away   (Diagram 8-2)
- In   (Diagram 8-3)
- Leave a spot, replace a spot
- Replacement
- Circle   (Diagram 8-4)
- Yankee(Diagram 8-5)
- Rebel   (Diagram 8-6)

It is better to be too far apart than too close together.

DIAGRAM 8-2. AWAY

DIAGRAMS 8-3A & 8-3B. IN

DIAGRAM 8-4. CIRCLE

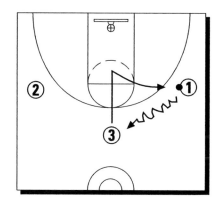

DIAGRAM 8-5. YANKEE

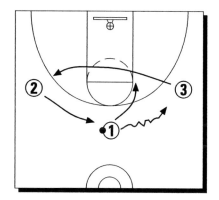

DIAGRAMS 8-6A & 8-6B. REBEL

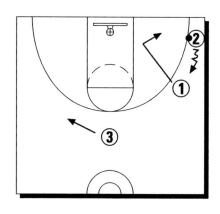
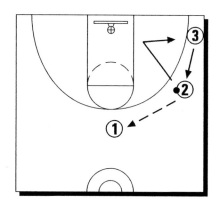

DIAGRAMS 8-6C. REBEL

Inside sequences
- Hold—this helps post rebounding (Diagram 8-7)
- Over/under—This is done on ball movement left to right.
- Posts flash and hold on ball movement right to left. (Diagram8- 8)
- High-low (Diagram 8-9)
- Stepping out (Diagram 8-10)

DIAGRAM 8-7. HOLD

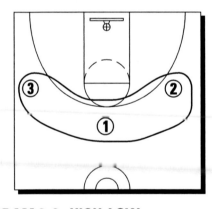

DIAGRAM 8-8. POSTS FLASH & HOLD

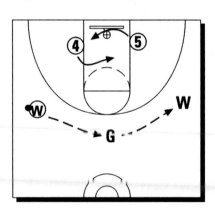

DIAGRAM 8-9. HIGH-LOW

DIAGRAM 8-10. STEPPING OUT

Plays

Do you want a wing out situation? Then use an interior screen. (Diagram 8-11)

Never run a play initially; move the defense first.

Double Back (Diagram 8-12)

Always have one non-shooter on the floor to run zone offense.

We like to attack the third, fourth, fifth sides of the zone.

DIAGRAM 8-11.

DIAGRAM 8-12.

Rebounding—On Offense

Three players rebound, while two players are back. They are designated this way:

    1 Fullback—he goes to the basket.

    1 Halfback—he goes to half-court and stops the ball.

    3 Tailbacks—they get their tail back.

Finally, come out of every time-out with a called play, a different alignment, or a change in defense.

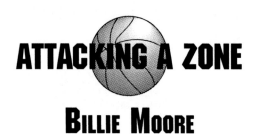

CHAPTER 9

ATTACKING A ZONE

BILLIE MOORE

Instead of having a different offense for each kind of zone, we try to teach some *concepts on attacking the zone.* Then you can use these in the type of offense you have depending on your personnel. First of all, we have some rules regardless of the type of offense we are running. We try to *revolve vs. a zone; cut vs. a man.* We try not to take a shot on the entry side without at least one ball reversal. We say we try not to, that means we don't usually do it. If you say that's a rule, then that's important to you. Then you must stick with it. If you ask players if they have ever taken a bad shot, most of them will *tell you no.*

We try to make every third or fourth pass into the post. We try to create a strongside and attack the helpside. You must teach your players how to make *pass fakes and shot fakes.* You must *teach* that. It is one of the hardest things to teach. Teaching someone to fake a shot is not natural. It is very difficult, but you must teach it. If you don't teach it, it's not going to happen. You can say to your players to fake a pass and they won't do anything any differently than when you have them as freshmen.

We run drills: *pass fake, shot fake, penetration.* We try to combine those things. If I have to teach fakes to my players, I know that you have to teach them to yours because I get your players. We try to set up our best perimeter player to stretch the defense. We try to go initially away from our best post player and then come back. That's *setting up strongside and attacking weakside.* I want to give you some ideas of what we try to do with our players.

We try to teach the idea of reading the defense. Have you ever asked them who's guarding them if they are playing against a zone? Is it the baseline player or the top player against a zone? Is it the baseline player or the top player guarding you? Do you think it makes any difference to how you attack it? You bet it does. How are they going to learn it unless you teach them how to read the defense? And this is the age of the match-up. Your players must be able to read defenses. There are three things we can talk about with our perimeter people. We can take it off the baseline, loop it off the top, and dribble follow.

Let's use a 2-3 zone.

DIAGRAM 9-1.

Let's start with a 1-4. Player 1 passes to 3. What are you going to teach 3 to read? Who guards 3, X1 or X3? It makes a difference. If X3 picks up 3, then the baseline is open. Now you have a chance of building something.

DIAGRAM 9-2.

3 will take it off the baseline with the dribble. X3 will probably follow. Now we can fill that baseline with 2, the shooter, or the short corner with 4, the post. Teach your players, if the baseline player picks up, take her away from where she came. That's *"take it off the baseline."*

DIAGRAM 9-3.

If X1 guards 3, take her away from where she came. *Dribble away.* 1 follows. 1 will be open. If not, 2 will be open on the weakside because I now have both guards on one side of the floor.

DIAGRAM 9-4.

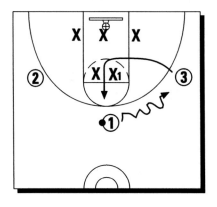

I can do the same concept with my perimeter, moving it off the top. 1 dribbles so that X1 guards her. 3 follows, dribble follow. Swing the ball and get the defense moving. Use a pass fake, shot fake, etc. At the same time your post players have some basic rules and concepts to follow. There are some things that go together; *seal out and flash, screen-in and postup, screen the middle usually followed by a flash, and step outs.* Of course, you still have the rotation and filling the high post, etc. Those are some of the concepts you can work with on the zone attack.

DIAGRAM 9-5. SEAL OUT

Seal out means that the post player has the opportunity to seal the defender. Anytime the post is being fronted, the post has the opportunity to seal when the ball is reversed. Finish the seal move with *flash or a postup* move. You must teach those two things together because players have a tendency to seal, then stand up, then post. When the player stands up, she releases the defensive player, so you must teach it together.

DIAGRAM 9-6. SCREEN IN AND POST.

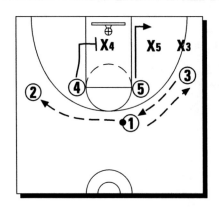

We are in the 1-4 screen-in on X4 on the reversal. And with the screen-in, you teach the postup. Who posts up? 5.

DIAGRAM 9-7.

What is X4 going to do on the pass to 2? Go around the screen. How many players screen and then just wait for the ball? Screen, go find 5 and postup. It works very well on an out-of-bounds play on the endline. It is very important for 4 to screen-in against X4 and take up space and postup 5. 5 is on the inside, on the ballside of the basket.

DIAGRAM 9-8.

I'm going to put an offense together with the two things I have just shown you. 1 dribbles toward 2, who loops. 5 screens in on X4. X4 will slide around then move out on 3.

DIAGRAM 9-9.

5 finds X5 and posts up, and will get the ball on the block. If it doesn't work, do the same thing on the other side.

DIAGRAM 9-10.

You can combine that with *take it off the baseline.* One thing I said post players can do is the step-out. That's the short corner. X5 will guard 5 on the step-out, 4 fills the high post and then 4 goes to the basket. The skip-pass is open from 3 to 2. We just combined taking it off the baseline with the step-out. You must teach your players to read defenses or else your post players will step-out when there is no place to go. They will step-out when the wing is picked up by the top guard. You can do combinations like looping it off the top, the skip-pass, screen-in and postup. Taking it off the baseline works well with the *step-out.*

DIAGRAM 9-11.

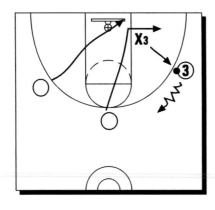

If you don't have a post player, take it off the baseline and run your best shooter through as a cutter to the short corner. When you take it off the baseline, you decide how you want to fill the corner. What does your personnel let you do? If you are a good coach, you will get your players to play basketball, not play plays. Play the game, don't play plays. You don't need plays for every occasion. Let them read it. Get both guards on one side of the floor with a dribble follow and something will be open on the backside.

DIAGRAM 9-12.

Let your post players screen the middle for each other. *Screen and then duck-in. Use screens against zones.* We don't use screens enough against zones. We think if we pass the ball long enough, we are going to get a shot.

DIAGRAM 9-13.

You can also use different kinds of entries. One thing we do is to dribble toward the wing, send 3 through, and 2 then fills so that the dribble follows; 3 will be open on the weakside for the shot.

Do you ever have to deal with combination defenses? The following are some simple rules. If you are attacking a box-in-one, we try to enter the ball to the high post. Have dribble penetration off of a pass fake or shot fake. We look for screens for the player being chased but we also use the screen-ins. Against a diamond-and-one, use a two-guard front. Bring one of your wings up. Use something with a baseline runner. Use this with taking it off the baseline. The runner can fill the short post. The runner can either be a wing or a top player. You can never go wrong entering the ball at the high post area against a Mickey Mouse defense.

CHAPTER 10

ATTACKING ZONES

KEVIN O'NEILL

Let me start by sharing with you what I consider to be the two keys to a good offense:

- Good spacing

- *Good shots*

You must fit your offense to your personnel. You better have rules for your players on offense. Chart your players' shots for the first two weeks of practice so you know what shots they can make. You always want to make sure your players know what a good shot is and that they take only good shots.

The first thing you need to attack a zone is a point guard who can recognize whether you're facing an even-or-odd front zone. *Every zone is a man-to-man that covers areas.* So, the first thing you need to decide is what areas each player covers. We want to attack the areas where two players' area of responsibility intersects.

DIAGRAM 10-1.

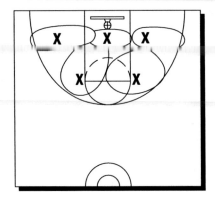

We use the dribble more against the zone than against man. I discourage the use of the dribble against a man defense. In our man offense, we have a rule that if you take more than two dribbles, you've overused it. Second, we like to force two men to guard three so we always emphasize the *concept of triangles.*

DIAGRAM 10-2.

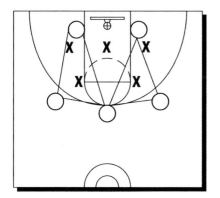

Third, we always want to attack from *behind the zone.*

DIAGRAM 10-3.

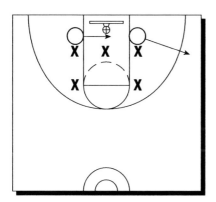

As the ball moves, the back of the zone changes. Because of this, we always want someone coming from behind so the zone has to worry and be aware of this.

DIAGRAM 10-4

We tell our players to attack the front of the zone, but to *score from behind.* We stress attacking the inside shoulder of the zone defender with the dribble. We also tell our big men to attack the inside shoulder of the defender and attack the zone from behind.

DIAGRAM 10-5.

We also attempt to place our quickest player against the other team's slowest player. The other team's slowest player is usually playing under the basket. We run what we call *guard through.*

DIAGRAM 10-6.

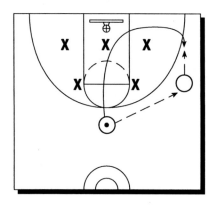

We get our point guard to pass and cut through to the corner on the ballside. We then get the ball to the corner and allow our point guard to attack the other team's forward. We place our best shooter on the side against the other team's weakest defender. We also place our best post up player against the other team's softest defender.

If playing against a pressure zone, we want to use the dribble.

DIAGRAM 10-7.

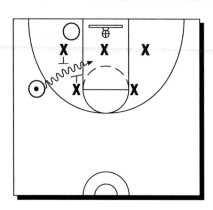

We want our players to *drive to the paint.* If you don't do this, they'll force you further from the basket. When playing against a passive zone, we use the dribble to get the ball to the baseline to flatten the zone and *reverse the ball.*

DIAGRAM 10-8.

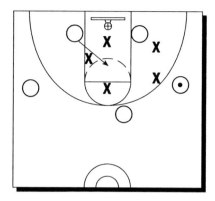

This goes *against our rule* of driving at the inside shoulder, but it is important to flatten this type of zone out if you want to defeat it. We stress using *ball fakes* against a pressure zone. We tell our players: "Fake a pass, make a pass." The only time we reverse the ball quickly, without using a ball fake, is when the off guard is out of position pressuring and we can get an open shot.

DIAGRAM 10-9.

Otherwise, we *dribble penetrate* before we reverse the ball. We also stress to our player at the point that he cannot pass the ball back to the side the ball came from until he has taken the ball past the center of the floor.

We want to force the zone to move. We also tell our players they must be shot ready. By this we mean that they should have their knees bent, the off-leg forward, and hands up ready to catch the ball. This little thing can mean the difference between getting a good shot or no shot or a forced shot. We tell our post players when they come to the ball and catch it, they have two options. They are:

- catch and shoot or
- throw the ball in the direction from which they came

DIAGRAM 10-10.

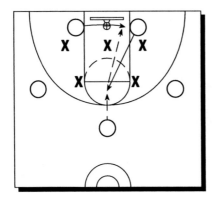

We don't want the post ever catching the ball and returning it to the passer. When we throw the ball to the post in the *short corner*, the other post is to *cut to the block* on the ballside.

We do this because it puts pressure on the defensive forward and center to decide who they should cover.

DIAGRAM 10-11.

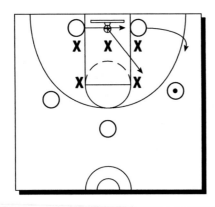

If the ball is passed to a post at the low position, we want the *offside post* to cut to the high post on the ballside looking for a pass from his teammate.

DIAGRAM 10-12

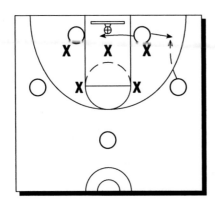

We tell the low post to make the pass and flare to the basket. We do this because most defensive post players tend to get lax when their man passes the ball and this makes them susceptible to the offensive post cutting in front of the defense for a pass and easy basket.

DIAGRAM 10-13.

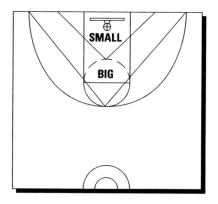

Post players are told to play *big triangle or small triangle.* When we have a good shooting post player, we allow him to play the *big triangle* area. When we have poor shooting post players, we allow them to run the *small triangle* area only.

DIAGRAM 10-14.

The first way we try to attack a zone is off our secondary break. We have the point guard bring the ball down moving to one side or the other. 2 and 3 fill the wing positions, 5 cuts to the box away from the ball, and 4 fills the weakside guard spot. 1 looks to 3, but reverses the ball to 4 who then passes to 2. 5 rolls away from the ball, and 4 cuts in the middle looking for a pass from 2.

DIAGRAM 10-15.

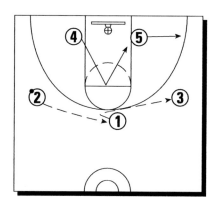

If this isn't open, 1 comes across to the ball and 2 *reverses* it to 1. 3 cuts up to the off-guard position and receives a pass from 1. 5 cuts to the *short corner*, 3 looks to hit 5, and 4 cuts high and comes to the *box* on the *ballside* looking for a dump in by 5.

DIAGRAM 10-16.

We like to run a 3 out, 2 in set, but if one of our post players is a good outside shooter, we run what we call *"4 Out."* 1 brings the ball to 4's side and passes to 3 on the wing. 4 rolls away to the offside elbow, and 5 rolls low to the ballside.

DIAGRAM 10-17.

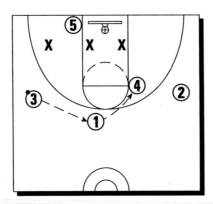

3 looks inside to 5 and reverses to 1. Player 1 then hits 4 at the offside elbow for the 15' jumper.

DIAGRAM 10-18.

This complies with our principle that we start away from our good shooter and then come back to him.

A play we ran successfully at Arizona is the *Corner Call.* No matter what zone you face, this play will get you a shot. We are in our 1-2-2 set. 1 brings the ball down and passes to 3. 4 cuts to the corner and receives a pass from 3. Upon passing to 4, 3 cuts to the box that 4 vacated. While this is happening, 2 moves down to stack with 5.

DIAGRAM 10-19.

4 returns the ball to 1 and moves to screen the defensive forward. At the same time, 5 moves to screen the defensive center. 2 cuts off 4's screen to the corner, and 3 cuts off 5's screen moving for the offside wing. 1 now should have a pass to 2 or 3 for an open shot.

DIAGRAM 10-20.

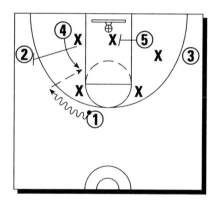

If the defensive forward would slip over 4's screen, we have 1 drive toward wing and 4 roll to the mid-post. At the same time 5 sets his screen on the defensive center. 4 now has a short jumper or a pass out to 3 for an open jump shot.

DIAGRAM 10-21.

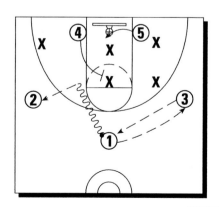

Sometimes, we'll screen the top of the zone when we take the ball away from the best shooter.

DIAGRAM 10-22.

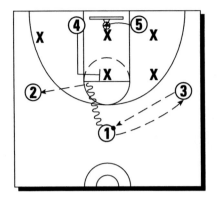

1 brings the ball down and passes to 3, going away from 2 (who is one of our better shooters). 3 reverses the ball to 1 and 4 moves up to screen the offside guard. 1 dribbles off this screen driving at the defensive forward. 5 ducks in on 1's dribble to occupy the defensive center. 2 sets at the wing and waits for 1's pass out for the open jumper.

DIAGRAM 10-23.

It seems that whenever we wanted to get a three-point shot, we could never do it, so we came up with the following play. 1 gets the ball from 3 on the reversal and drives at the guard who has moved out to guard him. As he makes this drive, 2 cuts off 1 to the top of the key. As 2 moves by 1, 1 turns and hands 2 the ball for the three-point shot.

I hope, in some way, the ideas I have shared with you will help you successfully attack the zones you will face in your league or conference.

CHAPTER 11

ZONE OFFENSE

KEVIN O'NEILL

Our strategy for attacking a zone defense is based on several points of emphasis we feel are important for good execution. Three of our key weapons on offense were, in the past, considered not to be fundamentally sound; *dribble penetration, setting picks, and using skip-passes.* However, with the implementation of the *match-up zone* and other adjustments that have been made in zones over the years, we feel that utilizing these weapons is *essential* for a consistent offense.

The basic ideas we try to emphasize against a zone, regardless of what specific offensive set we run, are as follows:

- *Penetration*—Dribble penetration into the *gaps* is an effective way of *drawing* two defenders to the ball. This sets up a four-on-three advantage for the rest of the offense, and if they move to *spot up* on the perimeter and *post-up* hard inside, it will lead to openings.

- *Set picks*—Zone defenders generally have vision on the ball, but not necessarily on a man. This leaves them vulnerable to *blind-side picks.*

- *Utilize skip-passes*—Skip or *cross-court* passes give the offense more options and are essential in attacking the weak side of a zone.

- *Attack inside, then out*—Look to get the ball inside first. This will cause the defense to collapse, which will, in turn, *open up* the perimeter.

- *Crash the boards*—One of the primary weaknesses of a zone defense is the confusion on *box-out* assignments. Take advantage of this! Two of three rebounds fall on the side opposite the shot—concentrate on the weakside.

- *Keep it simple*—Execution is the key. It isn't *what* you run, so much as *how* you run it. Know your options and how to execute them.

- *Use the three-pointer*—When spotting up for a shot near the three-point line, be *behind* it. Remember 33 percent from three = 50 percent from two. Don't ignore this weapon. Also, *longer shots* create *longer rebounds* and more second shot opportunities.

- *Read the defense*—If there is pressure on the perimeter, attack inside and vice versa.

- *Use ball fakes*—Fakes can cause a zone to *shift*; fake one way, then pass the other.

- *Be patient*—Screening, penetrating, and having good ball movement will eventually cause a zone to *break down* and lead to an easy basket. Be patient and shots will come.

Against any type of zone defense, we run a three-out, two-in *"freelance"* offense. Using the *"freelance"* enables us to stay with the same offense regardless of the types of zone we're facing. We make adjustments in the areas we try to attack depending on the zone, but we stay with the *same basic principles*.

THE THREE-OUT, TWO-IN FREELANCE OFFENSE

Positions	Diagrams			
1 - Point Guard	Offensive Player	1,2,3	Cut	
2 - Shooting Guard	Defender	X	Drive	
3 - Small Forward Pass	Screen	⊢	Dribble	
4 - Power Forward	Player w-ball	③		
5 - Center	Pass	- - →		

The *"three-out, two-in"* refers to the three players we use out on the *perimeter* and the two big men who work *inside*. The perimeter players are all three *interchangeable* as are our two post men. The perimeter and the inside players have two separate sets of rules they must follow.

DIAGRAM 11-1.

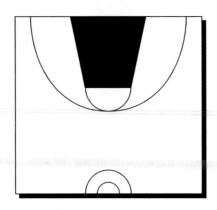

Our two inside players work primarily in the shaded region. On occasion we will pop a big man out on the perimeter to *reverse* the ball or to take an *open jump shot*, but most of the time they stay inside. The perimeter players stay outside of the shaded area except for drives and cuts through the lane.

In order to add some structure and keep things organized, we have the following *specific rules* for our big men to follow:

- *Keep good spacing*, approximately 10-15 feet apart, to prevent one defender from guarding both players.

- *Look to score.* When they catch the ball inside, their *first option* is to score. If they are scoring threats, it will cause the defense to *collapse around them, creating openings* on the perimeter.

- *Work to get the ball.* It is important for them to work hard to get the ball. *Flash* to openings, seal the defenders, and remain *active*—never stand still.

- Cut to the basket. When one post man catches the ball, the other should cut to the basket. This puts him in good rebounding position if the shot goes up, and if the defense double-teams the post, he may be open for layups.

- *Screen for the weakside perimeter man.* This can get the perimeter man a jump shot; see Diagram 11-2.

DIAGRAM 11-2.

If the defender *slips* the screen, the post man meets the next defender in the middle of the lane and seals him on his back in order to receive the ball inside, as in Diagrams 11-3 and 11-4:

DIAGRAM 11-3.   ## DIAGRAM 11-4.

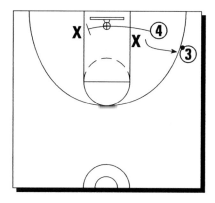   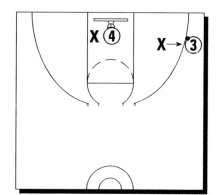

- *Rebound.* When a shot goes up, both post players should always go hard to the boards. The ball side post should spin to the middle, and the other should work for position near the offside block, as in Diagram 11-5.

DIAGRAM 11-5.

It's important for the post players to screen, cut, flash to the openings, and rebound. They must *vary* what they do and never stop working.

Our three perimeter players have a separate set of objectives:

- *Penetrate the gaps.* This will bring two defenders together, leaving a four-on-three advantage for the other offensive players.

- *Keep spacing.* The players should stay at least fifteen feet apart. If one perimeter player drives toward another, he should *flare* away and spot up on the perimeter.

- *Slide the perimeter.* When the ball is passed inside, the perimeter players should slide around the outside looking for the open areas.

- *Rebound.* The weakside perimeter man should *crash* the boards hard after every shot. In the past, we have assigned one specific perimeter player to go to the boards while the other two get back on defense, but this should only be done if one player is clearly a superior rebounder.

These sets of rules and objectives help to add structure, but they don't restrict the players from using their creativity.

AREAS TO ATTACK A ZONE

Whatever zone a team plays, the *weaknesses* are always in the *seams* and in the gray areas. By seams, we mean the area between defenders. When we refer to the gray areas, we're talking about the areas on the perimeter that make it difficult to determine which defender should guard the ball.

For example, the gray areas and seams are as follows in Diagrams 11-6 and 11-7:

DIAGRAM 11-6.

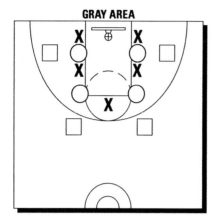

DIAGRAM 11-7.

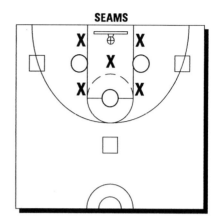

ATTACKING THE GRAY AREAS

By catching the ball in the *gray areas*, several problems are created for the defense. There will be an instant of confusion as to whose responsibility the man is. Sometimes both defenders will pick him up, which creates other openings, and sometimes both defenders will *stand back* and watch, leaving an open shot.

DIAGRAM 11-8.

If they do *communicate* well, and one man picks up the ball, the offensive player should take one or two dribbles away from that defender's area to try to distort the zone and create openings. For example, if the high man picks up three, he would drive toward the baseline.

DIAGRAM 11-9.

If they try to *switch* defenders, they must bring two defenders to the ball momentarily.

DIAGRAM 11-10.

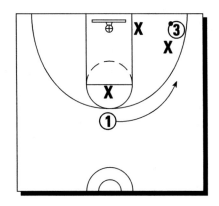

With proper spacing and a good pass, the defense is very vulnerable at this time. For example, if 1 comes over to keep 15' spacing, he will be open.

ATTACKING THE SEAMS

DIAGRAM 11-11.

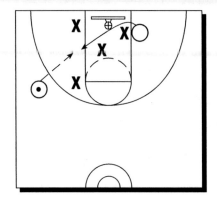

There are *two ways* in which to *attack the seams*. The big man can *flash* into the seams to receive the ball, or the perimeter men may *penetrate* into the seams. When the big men flash to the seams, they should try to go behind the line of vision of the defenders. By doing this, it will keep the defense from closing the gap.

When a perimeter man penetrates into the seams, he should *look to score* if the seam doesn't close. If the seam closes, there will be a four-on-three advantage on the rest of the court, so he should hit the open man. If our offense becomes stagnant, we run a play to *force* movement and screens.

THE "CORNER PLAY"

DIAGRAM 11-12.

The point guard should recognize when we are having difficulty. He then passes to the wing and calls, *"Corner!"* The call signals for our closest big man to pop to the corner and receive the ball. The other wing and post go to the weakside block.

DIAGRAM 11-13.

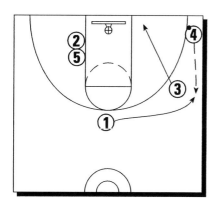

After 3 passes to the corner, he posts up on the block and 1 fills the spot 3 vacated. 4 then passes out to 1.

Here is where we get the best action:

DIAGRAM 11-14.

The point guard drives the ball to the center of the floor. If not open to score, he looks for 2 or 3, who cross and are coming off baseline screens simultaneously.

DIAGRAM 11-15.

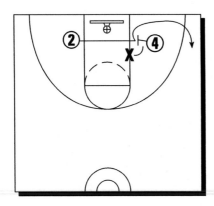

DIAGRAM 11-16.

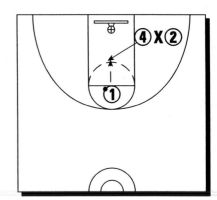

In Diagrams 11-15 and 11-16, the point guard must see the whole floor and make the *best* decision. If the defender slips through the screen, the post should step toward the ball and receive a pass to score.

DIAGRAM 11-17.

DIAGRAM 11-18.

If the point guard delivers the ball to one of the wing players who isn't open for a shot, the wing player *drives away* from the baseline, the post man pops to the *corner*, and we are back into our play. Diagrams 11-17 and 11-18.

DIAGRAM 11-19.

We also run a *lob play*. We call this play from a timeout situation to catch the defense off guard. 4 pops to the corner and receives a pass from 3, 2 goes to the weakside block, and 5 posts up on the block.

DIAGRAM 11-20.

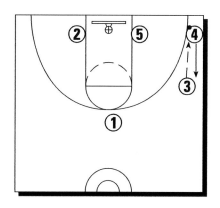

4 passes back to 3 and steps toward his pass to bring the low defender up higher.

DIAGRAM 11-21.

Next, 3 passes to 1. Player 1 drives to the left to improve his *passing angle* and to make the defense shift. Then, 5 screens the defender closest to the middle of the lane and 2 cuts through the lane and screens the defender who had been guarding 4 in the corner. 4 cuts to the basket looking for the *lob pass.*

NOTE: When 2 cuts across to set the back pick, he should come from the baseline side to prevent the defender from seeing the screen coming.

DIAGRAM 11-22.

If the defense sags into the block area to prevent the lob, 3 *flares* to the corner looking for a three-pointer.

Attacking a zone is simple. There are just a few concepts that we try to teach, and the rest comes down to *reading the defense and execution.*

CHAPTER 12

ATTACKING ZONES

BOB PATTON

Ask yourself—Why are they playing a zone?

- Are they trying to protect someone?
- Is their overall defense poor?

Principles:

- Make someone guard the ball
- Put people behind someone
- Get perimeter players to step up into shooting areas
- Force the zone to defend both sides of the floor
- Overload—swing to overload
- Drive the seams of the zone
- Best way to beat a zone is to rebound — get second shots

We feel the most important thing is to screen the zone:

- It distorts the zone and puts someone slightly out of position
- Other people can probably get more open

All zones look alike once the ball goes to the corner:

- Basic continuity (Diagrams 12-1, 12-2 and 12-3)
- Wing away (Diagram 12-4)
- Push (Diagrams 12-5, 12-6 and 12-7)
- Vs. 3-2 Matchup or 1-3-1 (Diagrams 12-8 through 12-11)
  Attack the man they are trying to protect in your zone.
- Liberty vs. 2-3 especially (Diagrams 12-12, 12-13 and 12-14)
- 33 (3 for 3) (Diagrams 12-15 and 12-16)

DIAGRAM 12-1. BASIC ALIGNMENT 1-3-1

Enter to either side and go to a corner. 2 goes through, 5 cuts off his back.

DIAGRAM 12-2.

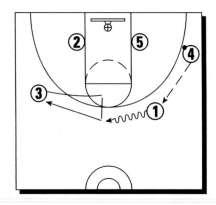

4 passes to 1, who dribbles to the top of the circle. 3 moves to the top of the circle and then back toward his original spot.

DIAGRAM 12-3.

1 takes two hard dribbles to allow 3 time to fade.

DIAGRAM 12-4.

4 and 5 double-screen for 2. Options: Lob to 5. Player 4 cuts up the middle for pass.

DIAGRAM 12-5.

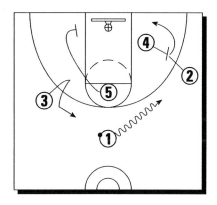

1 dribbles to 2. Player 2 goes behind the screen from 4 and 5.

DIAGRAM 12-6.

Swing the ball to 2.

DIAGRAM 12-7.

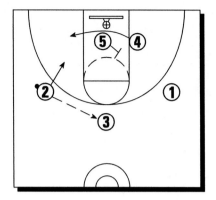

5 back-screens the middle of the zone. 4 follows the cutter, 2, and either 2 or 4 are open. 5 must seal by screening the middle low man in the zone.

DIAGRAM 12-8.

3 pops to the middle.

DIAGRAM 12-9.

1 must screen the zone. 5 pins the elbow man and 3 screens diagonally for 2 breaking to the elbow.

DIAGRAM 12-10.

If nothing develops, 3 screens and flares to the corner.

DIAGRAM 12-11.

5 can dive after a back-screen.

DIAGRAM 12-12

1 dribbles at 2, who goes to the corner. 3 should be a good passer. 5 goes weakside. 1 passes back out to 3.

DIAGRAM 12-13.

2 flashes and goes right through to the 3-point area.

DIAGRAM 12-14.

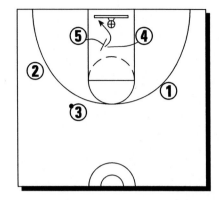

4 flashes to the middle, right behind the cut. 4 takes one big step, not a running step, to get balance. 5 back-screens for a lob to 4 going to the basket. If they sag to protest the lob, fake and pass to 2 for a 3-point shot.

DIAGRAM 12-15. "33"

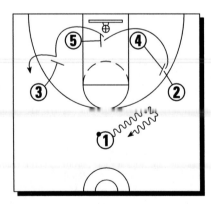

Penetrate and pitch (3 for 3). We are going to back-screen 2's man. Use a back-screen (4), a down-screen (3), and a cross-screen (5). 1 dribbles toward 2 and reverses back.

DIAGRAM 12-16. REVERSE BACK-OUT.

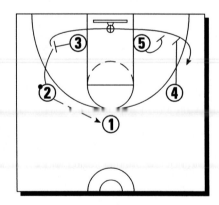

3 back-screens for 2. Players 4 and 5 double-screen for 2.

CHAPTER 13

TWELVE RULES FOR A ZONE OFFENSE

SONNY SMITH

The zone offense isn't pretty. You never draw it up; nobody likes their zone offense. So, let's develop a little philosophy here. You must decide *where* you want to *attack* that zone. Do you want to attack on the strongside? I doubt very seriously that there are many people who want to attack on the strongside. Why? Because you are going to shoot too soon. My preference would be to attack the backside. If I had a preference beyond that, I would attack the backside block. Why? Because I would prefer to attack the zone from the *inside out* as opposed to the *outside in.* Because that big guy can throw over the zone, skip the ball for you, throw diagonal passes, attack the zone on a diagonal and you can be a lot more successful going with the *inside out attack.* Now, I am going to set my offense to get the rebound.

Every night you strive, pray, and hope to shoot 50%. Anytime you've shot less than 50%, you've missed more than half of your shots. Why don't you design the offense to get the rebound, knowing your opponent will miss more than 50% of their shots most nights. Next thing you must decide is whether to move with the ball, to move people, or are you going to do a combination? If you do a strong evaluation of your people, you will find out that some kids can shoot on the move, some kids can't. So, why should you set up shots for them to catch the ball and shoot it on the move?

You might be better off to stand them in the *gaps* on the *perimeter* and use them as *catch and shoot players.* Don't design your offense on who can cut pretty, design it on whether your players are catch and shoot players or whether they can catch the ball on the move and shoot it. Probably you want a combination of both. The last thing, before we get into the rules, guard against being pretty. Don't make that thing flow so that it looks good on paper. Evaluate it on the number of *open shots* you get and on the number of second shots that you can get. Then set up your zone offense and depend on your offensive rebounding to help you.

At this point, I am going to set 12 rules, then, in the next chapter, I will draw a zone offense using those 12 rules. If you have an offense with these 12 rules in it, you have an effective zone offense; you have done your job. Another question is, are you going to *attack for three?* Some coaches have had a hard time deciding whether they are going to be the same type of coach they were before the three-point shot or not. Shoot the three! And teach your kids to rebound long rebounds.

RULE 1: PENETRATE THE GAPS.

Do you penetrate the gaps with the dribble? In the NBA today, 90% of the offense is penetrate the gaps and pitch. Get two defenders on the ball and throw the ball to the open man.

DIAGRAM 13-1.

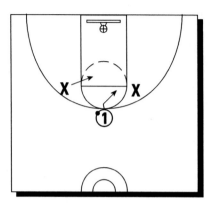

Here is a two-guard front zone. I am going to attack this middle gap with the dribble. You must make a serious coaching decision on how you *attack the gap*. Do you attack the center of the gap? Do you drive at the inside shoulder of one of the defenders? Two things are important. To distort the gap, I would *penetrate toward the inside shoulder* of one of the defenders. I will go into the gap with a *saddle-dribble* type of technique. I will turn sideways. The reason is that I don't open my body so both defenders have a chance to deflect. Set your offense to cut down on the number of turnovers. If I attack the inside shoulder, I fully occupy one of the defenders and draw the other over several steps opening up a wing pass or a post pass. If you go up the center of the gap, you leave yourself nothing to throw to except the wings.

RULE 2: SCREENING THE ZONE.

If I had my choice of zone offense and only could pick one, I would attack every zone out of a 1-4, or a 1-2-2, regardless of whether it was a one- or two-guard front. I would set the offense and attempt to flow into the gaps instead of having a different offense for every defense.

DIAGRAM 13-2.

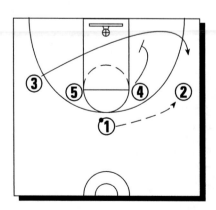

The decision you must make is are you going to screen the strongside of the zone for a shot, or are you going to screen the weakside of the zone for a shot? Every chance I have, I will screen the weakside of the zone. Anytime you attack the strongside, they have more defenders in the area than you have offensive people. So you want to *screen the backside, throw and cut through.*

DIAGRAM 13-3.

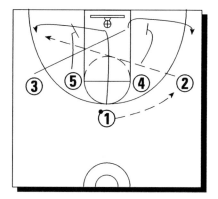

1 passes to 2; 3 cuts through. 1 cuts through and out. 5 screens the backside of the zone.

DIAGRAM 13-4.

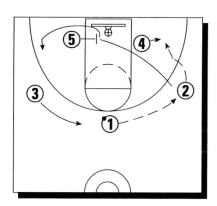

As he picks the backside, we fill each of these positions with someone. Keep in mind that this is not a play. Never look at the player that you are going to throw the ball to.

DIAGRAM 13-5.

Always look at the screener. Tell your players to set the pick and *run to the ball.* We are looking to hit the screener because we want to attack from the inside out. *Get the ball to the picker.*

RULE 3: THE DRIBBLE RULE.

Remember this is not an offense, this is a rule. If you have a dribble rule, you must have a straight rule.

DIAGRAM 13-6.

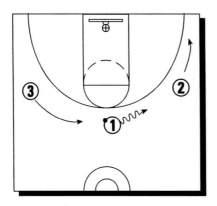

My *straight rule* is, if I dribble toward you, you will *run away* from me. If I am behind the ball, I follow the ball. That sinks the backside of the zone, and 3 will get a quick shot from the reversal. That's a good three-point shot. Does your dribble rule have 2 clear all the way through and 1, 2, and 3 replace each other? How far do you want your people spaced? Don't always go with that 15' to 18' spacing that some-one told you, because your kids may not be able to throw anything longer than a 15' pass. You determine your spacing based on the ability of your kids to throw a quick *hard pass* back across the zone.

RULE 4: FLASHES.

That's different from cuts. Flashes are short, *quick bursts* up into the center, the heart of the defense from behind the zone.

DIAGRAM 13-7.

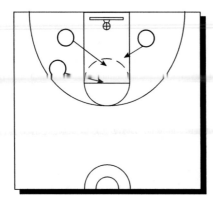

I prefer that those short quick flashes be done on a *diagonal.* I want to get you thinking. Build your own offense. Some have these cuts all the way through the zone into the gap areas. I don't like that.

RULE 5: CUTTERS.

Cutters are different from flashers.

DIAGRAM 13-8.

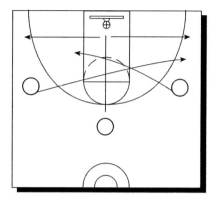

Cutters are going from one side of the court to the other; *down and out.* Do you have cutters through the zone? If so, I make the decision based on which way I want my cutters to go. If I were using cutters, I would go from *strongside to weakside* as opposed to the opposite. Why? There are less defenders on the weakside, and *rapid ball reversal* will get you a quick shot on the backside of the zone with less defenders. So, go from *strong to weak.*

RULE 6: JUMP PASSES.

DIAGRAM 13-9.

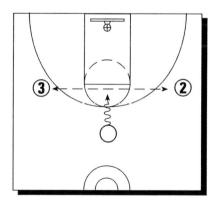

I mentioned the word "stationary." Do you stand your people in the gaps? You can let all of the movement be done by the inside people. This was started by Cal Luther. Cal Luther throws jump passes. He would penetrate the gap, jump in the air above the zone and made the jump pass to the perimeter men. Never do it against a man defense. Consider a jump pass in your perimeter stand.

RULE 7: THE STEP OUT.

DIAGRAM 13-10.

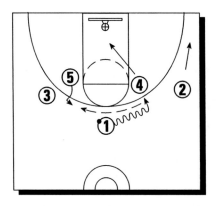

This is one of the important rules. If you play against a zone, you may be playing against a match-up zone most of the time. Did you ever hear anyone ask, "What are your fears in basketball?" The fears are attacking the press, attacking a match-up, and gimmick defenses. They want you to play a straight man or a regular zone. If you are going to play against match-ups, you must do something like Diagram 13-10. You must step people from *inside* the zone to the *outside* to give you four on the perimeter. Make sure that you have four on the perimeter if you attack a match-up, it is the most difficult match-up there is. This is especially true if a player steps out from inside the zone.

DIAGRAM 13-11.

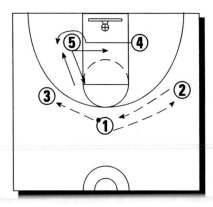

Let me say this again, this is not an offense. 1 passes to 2. Player 5 flashes to the elbow. The ball is reversed from 2 to 1 to 3. Player 5 slides down to the block and 4 comes off 5's rear end. Cross them off of each other's rear end. What does that do? That *pinches the zone* and opens up the perimeter shot.

RULE 9: FILL THE VACUUM.

DIAGRAM 13-12.

We can fill the vacuum off of the dribble or the pass. 1 dribbles toward 2, who cuts through and 3 follows. That's filling the vacuum on the perimeter.

DIAGRAM 13-13.

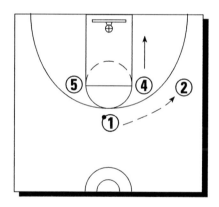

You also fill it on the inside. 1 passes to 2, 4 slides down, and 5 fills the hole.

RULE 10: DENNY CRUM *ATTACKS* A ZONE AS WELL AS ANYBODY.

DIAGRAM 13-14.

When you first see him, it doesn't look like he's doing anything. He stands his biggest player, 5, behind the zone. He plays 4 in the gap and the shooters on the perimeter. He is now second or third in the country in three-point shooting. Not the number attempted, but the percentage made. He stands his big man there. Give him the ball there and he is up looking over the zone. He is throwing skip-passes across the zone, hitting cutters going down the middle, hitting players filling behind the cutters. So he attacks with a standing player behind the zone, a big man. No matter what type of zone you are playing, who is going to block out big 5? No one can block him out if he runs in to rebound or runs inside and seals. If you are shooting 3's, he will run farther to rebound. Long rebounds are his.

RULE 11: SKIP-PASSES.

DIAGRAM 13-15.

We just showed it with 5. This is 2 skip-passing to 3. This is the fastest way to move a ball against a zone. When you attack a zone, and the ball hits your hand, where do you put it? Do you put it in the triple threat, do you chin it, or do you put it above your head? You must develop a *passing philosophy.* Teach every player how to fake a shot, fake a pass, and fake a drive. During a game, do combinations of these fakes, depending on the abilities of your team. Which way would you do it? I know I would *fake* the shot first. If the ball hits my hands, I am not going to hold the ball low. I want it up in *shooting position.* I would only use the *shot fake* and the *pass fake* because I want to be able to skip it, every time, to get it back across the zone.

RULE 12: DIAGONALS.

DIAGRAM 13-16.

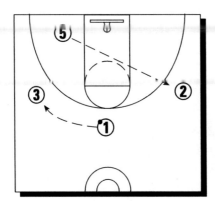

Make a pass to 5 in the short corner and have him pass to 2. That is a diagonal. Work on diagonals. 1 can make a diagonal pass to 3.

CHAPTER 14

ZONE OFFENSE

SONNY SMITH

We would prefer to line up in a 1-2-2 or a 1-4. Let's use a 1-2-2.

DIAGRAM 14-1. FIRST MOVE

1 passes to 2. Player 5 flashes to the high-post area. 4 holds for two seconds and then goes to the short corner. Anytime the ball goes to one of the inside people, we have *a high-post rule and a low-post rule.* If the pass goes to the *high post*, it is the high-post rule, etc.

The rest of the offense is based on *perimeter play.* We want to get the ball inside any time we can. We are going to do the *perimeter rule* first. 1 takes two steps in the direction that he passes.

DIAGRAM 14-2.

We want 2, 3, and 5 in a line. That will make the defensive guard drop down to guard 5. Player 1 will get the return pass from 2, who dribbles away hard.

DIAGRAM 14-3.

When 1 dribbles away, we are in a *modified dribble rule* at this time. 3 runs to an opening and sets up for a *catch and shoot situation. Next rule,* 5 steps out from inside. Now we have 4 on the perimeter.

DIAGRAM 14-4.

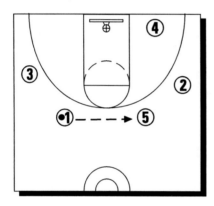

The reason for the dribble was to pull the defense over. 1 now passes back to 5.

DIAGRAM 14-5.

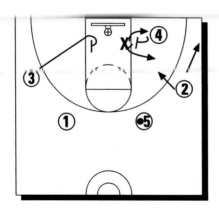

The ball is in the hands of 5. Player 4 is in the *short corner,* 3 is in the *dead corner.*

As the ball starts toward 5, the action by the other people begins. 3 runs the baseline to get inside rebounding position. 4 pins the deepest defender in the zone with his screen. 2 sets up for a shot depending on which way the defender tries to move. If the lowest defender in the zone goes around the bottom, he slides high. Normally they will go over the top, and 2 slides low. If he stays behind, he is ready for the 3-point shot. Make sure that your two best shooters are 2 and 3. After 4 sets the pick, he steps to the ball.

DIAGRAM 14-6.

4 can catch the ball in the seam of the zone. But suppose that 5 passed to 2. The only time he would throw to 2 is if 2 is open for the 3-point shot. As 5 passes to 2, he cuts into the heart of the zone. 1 fills that area for another 3-point possibility because the defender will either be fronting the high post or moving with the cutter.

DIAGRAM 14-7.

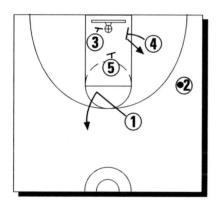

2 has the ball. 4 has picked and posted. 5 has cut inside. 3 is in position to rebound the backside, 1 is in a position to shoot a 3-point shot. If 2 shoots the ball, 3, 4, and 5 have the rebounding triangle. Who gets the long rebound? 2 moves to the elbow, 1 moves for the long rebound, but is really thinking "back." Let's go back to where 4 screens that low man on the zone. When 4 picks, my first move is to take *two steps* to the ball. If the ball is passed to 2, 4 screens the defensive post man. Now 4 is in a position to score with the pass coming in on the baseline side. He has sealed the middle defender on the zone.

DIAGRAM 14-8.

Let's go to the backside. Remember we have designed the offense to get the rebound. Remember that when you are working on an offensive rebound vs. a zone, you are attempting a lot of long 3-point shots. The ball is going to bounce longer. 2 passes to 1; 1 reverses the ball to 3. This is the only time we make a long, extended pass. Now we use a post "X", 5 breaks down to the block, preferably about the block. 4 cuts off of his rear end to the open area. There's your X move.

DIAGRAM 14-9.

5 holds for a 2-second count, and goes to the *short corner.* Never throw the ball to a man cutting to the short corner. Make sure that he is in the corner with his feet facing mid-court before you throw the pass. Now you have a man behind the zone. Make the man behind the zone work both sides of the floor. 1 fills behind the pass.

DIAGRAM 14-10.

When 3 passes to 1, 1 dribbles away extremely fast toward the other side. 4 steps out from inside the zone.

DIAGRAM 14-11.

3 is setting to shoot. 5 is in the short corner, 4 has stepped out on the perimeter; 1 has the ball; 2 ran to the corner when 1 dribbled toward him. 2 is a threat to shoot the three point shot. The zone is now spread. 1 passes back to 4, and everybody goes into action. 2 runs the baseline to rebound on the inside. 2 cuts around and under and comes back inside. 5 picks the only player who can cover 3. 3 will slide low, or slide high, or step up, catch and shoot. When 4 passes the ball, 4 cuts back inside looking for the return pass. 1 fills right behind 4 for the attempted three-point shot. I have a 6'9" Russian playing for me, and all he does is step out and shoot 3's. He can't make a layup, but he can shoot from the outside.

DIAGRAM 14-12.

We tell 4 to drive the ball to the goal. That's where the *penetrate and pitch* comes from. In European basketball, they always fill the area from which they have penetrated. 1 fills behind 4 as 4 has taken the defenders with him. 4 turns and passes back, and 1 shoots the three-point shot. That is the *gapping rule.*

DIAGRAM 14-13.

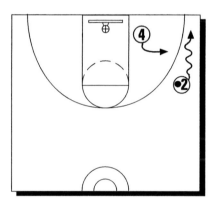

We work these types of drills. 2 has the ball; 4 is on the block. 2 drives to the baseline; 4 loops out.

DIAGRAM 14-14.

If 2 drives out, 4 loops toward the baseline into an open area.

DIAGRAM 14-15.

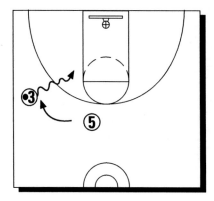

If you are on the perimeter and make a penetrating move, we fill behind on the loop.

DIAGRAM 14-16.

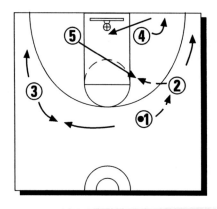

Here is the inside part now. This is the *high-post rule.* 1 passes to 2. Player 5 flashes to the high post. 4 holds for two seconds and goes to the *short corner.* Suppose 2 passed to 5.

DIAGRAM 14-17.

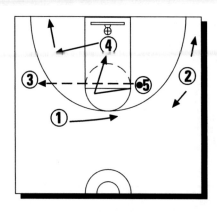

When the ball goes to the high-post man, the low post man crosses the basket either in front of, or behind, the defender — whichever is open. The wings slide into an open spot. *High-post rule: look low, look weakside, look strong.* Why weakside? Because there are less defenders over there. That is a skip-pass. 3 will be more open than anyone. Another part of this would be when 5 passes to 3. Player 4 is crossing the lane; 1 is filling the top area, and 2 slides. Say that you passed the ball to 3. The rule is, anytime a skip-pass occurs, don't cross. That's too slow. Come straight to the ball as quickly as you possibly can. You are into your offense. If the ball is thrown to 4 in the short corner, the rule is, high-post man dives at the basket. Wings slide into an opening. If the pass is made to a wing, both post men go to the ball.

DIAGRAM 14-18.

Suppose that 5 passes back to 1 and 1 starts dribbling away. 5 steps out.

DIAGRAM 14-19.

After that has occurred several times, the guard on that side will come out with 5 and try to steal the ball. Anytime that occurs, the skip-pass is open and you will get the better 3's on the skip-pass. 1 immediately looks for the skip. This offense was designed to get the rebound and was designed for three-point shooters. It was designed to step out on the perimeter so you can play against match-ups. What hurts a match-up more than anything else? *Screening the match-up.* Teach your people to react to the screen by coming to the ball, by *fading off the screen*, or by *curling off the screen.* The *fade* is the best way to shoot, not coming to the ball, but fading away.

CHAPTER 15

ZONE OFFENSIVE THEORIES

STEVE STEINWEDEL

Against the zone, the areas we would highlight in execution are:

- Throw skip-passes, but not skip-passes that are directly across the zone. (Diagrams 15-1 and 15-2)
- Set up in a different alignment each time down court. (Diagrams 15-3, 15-4 and 15-5)
- Utilize the baseline for cuts and passes.
- The pass and shot-fake.
- Ball reversal.

DIAGRAM 15-1.

DIAGRAM 15-2.

DIAGRAM 15-3.

DIAGRAM 15-4.

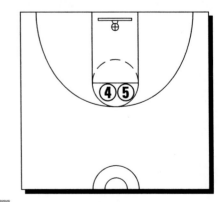

DIAGRAM 15-5.

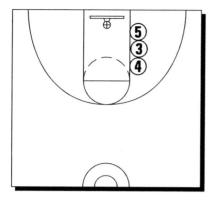

How do we use the dribble vs. the zone?

DIAGRAM 15-6.

The first thing we would do with the dribble is to penetrate the gaps of the zone. We want to force two players to play one and thus open an advantage someplace on the floor were we would have two of our players attacking one.

DIAGRAM 15-7.

The second thing we would do with the dribble is what is known as a freeze dribble. On the reversal of the ball, we would drive at the off guard to "freeze" him and open up our player on the wing for a shot or a pass into the post.

DIAGRAM 15-8.

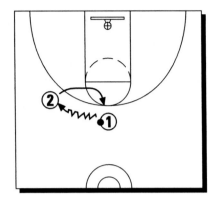

The third thing we would do with the dribble versus the zone would be to dribble off the top of the zone and then attack the gaps. We are attempting to get the zone to move and then reverse the ball to the offside.

DIAGRAM 15-9.

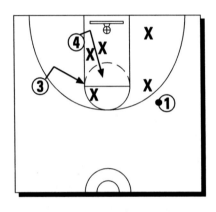

Another thing we do against a zone is to keep a man behind the zone. We want to have a man that slashes into the zone from behind. We might do this by flashing a post from behind the zone toward the ball on the top or by slashing the off wing toward the ball when it is on the wing. We like to put players behind the zone, down on the baseline, because it forces the zone to spread out. People choose to play zone either because they don't match up with your athletic ability and quickness, or they are attempting to contain your post. Because of this, the zone will be very compact. So by flashing players from behind the zone, you will cause it to expand or spread out.

DIAGRAM 15-10

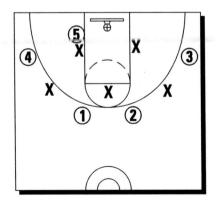

You can also attack the zone by distorting it through different alignments. Our basic rule in regard to this principle is that we place players in positions where we get the best numerical alignment. Against a 3-2 zone we line up with a numerical disadvantage on top and a numerical advantage on the bottom. Thus, we have two players occupying the strength of the zone while we attack the weak point of the zone with three players.

Another option we use in attacking zones is to screen the zone. We do this in a number of ways.

DIAGRAM 15-11.

One way is to screen the low part of the zone and use the skip-pass we talked about earlier. A second option in screening the zone is to screen the top of the zone.

You can screen the zone in various ways; see Diagrams 15-12, 15-13 and 15-14.

DIAGRAM 15-12.

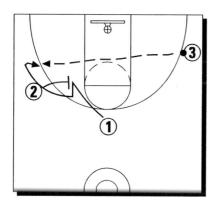

DIAGRAM 15-13.

DIAGRAM 15-14.

The next concept we teach in attacking zones is offensive rebounding. We, as coaches, need to teach the angles. What I mean by this is that we need to teach our players to know the angles of rebound. They need to read the shots and go get the ball. We, especially like to attack the offside from the shot with two rebounders.

The last concept we teach in attacking zones is the inside-out attack. By this, we mean that we stress to our players that we want to attack the inside of the zone first. We want to force the defense to collapse and expand. If we do this enough, we will open up shots on both the perimeter and in the post. A favorite move that we like to use in doing this is what we call a "step out post." An automatic move that we have when the ball is passed inside is that everytime a post man touches the ball, the other post always cuts to the basket, as in Diagrams 15-15, 15-16, and 15-17:

DIAGRAM 15-15.

DIAGRAM 15-16.

DIAGRAM 15-17.

Some things we do to teach our zone offense attack include:

- Show our players two or three alignments before practice and then demand that they use them all during practice. We also allow our players to be creative and come up with their own alignments.

- We demand that they be patient, recognize, and move against the zone. These are the most important things in attacking a zone.

- Stress that a player be in the ready position when catching the ball. This was called "catch and tuck" by Coach Wooden. We want our players to catch the ball with their feet facing the basket and be ready to shoot. The ball is to be kept tucked under their chin and they are to always step in to shoot upon catching the ball, even if they aren't really going to shoot. This teaches the concept of shot-fake.

- We stress that the players look to fast-break the zone as the first option in attacking it.

- We place restrictions on the zone offense, such as: the post man must touch the ball before a shot, two screens must be made before shooting, the ball must be reversed X times before a shot is taken.

- We overload the zone by moving our perimeter players either from the point position or offside wing to the corner position on the ball side. See Diagrams 15-18 and 15-19.

DIAGRAM 15-18.

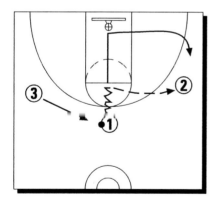

DIAGRAM 15-19.

CHAPTER 16

ZONE OFFENSIVE CONCEPTS

RICHARD WILLIAMS

In talking about offense, whether it is man-to-man or zone, I believe three things are vital: ball movement, player movement, and shot selection.

BALL MOVEMENT

How do you move the ball? Do you pass it or dribble it?

PLAYER MOVEMENT

I believe you can do four things against a zone with player movement:

- gap the zone
- cut against the zone
- slide to open areas vs. the zone
- screen the zone

SHOT SELECTION

How do you define shot selection? We determine it by a player's distance from the goal, the defensive pressure he's facing and the coach's feeling about his shooting potential. Some players you'll let take a three-pointer and some players you won't. If you are a coach and you can't dictate to your players what shots you want them taking and what ones you don't, then you might as well sit back and watch the game because your team is running the game, not you.

Another thing we add to these three, late in the game, is *time and score*. Different situations dictate what you consider a good shot. For example, with three minutes to play and up by three, you probably are not as apt to see a 20-footer as being the ideal shot you want, while being three points down might make you feel the 20-footer is a good shot.

BALL MOVEMENT VS. A ZONE

DIAGRAM 16-1.

We like to *dribble penetrate* against a zone. We tell our players to dribble into the gaps and force two to play one. Indiana is the best at doing this. We tell our players they should only need two dribbles to get into a gap. If they need more than two, they should pass. When dribbling into a gap, we want our players to make the two dribbles, come to a jump stop and look to pass.

DIAGRAM 16-2.

We also like to *dribble against a zone to "stretch it."* If we can get the bottom defender on a zone to move with the wing on the dribble, we will move a player into the baseline area and look to get it to him for the quick shot.

DIAGRAM 16-3.

In *passing versus a zone*, we stress the concept of inside-outside. Most coaches today don't leave the man who makes the pass into the post in the zone, because of the three-point shot. Instead, most teams send somebody from the weakside to help on the post. So, we instruct our post players to catch the ball and look opposite.

DIAGRAM 16-4.

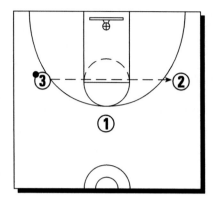

We also feel that the *skip-pass* is a good tool in ball movement against a zone.

DIAGRAM 16-5.

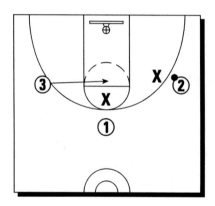

We like to have our weakside wing look to *cut* into the high post of the zone when it is open. We don't like to cut our weakside post into the zone because we don't feel this will help us in working our inside-outside philosophy of passing against the zone.

DIAGRAM 16-6

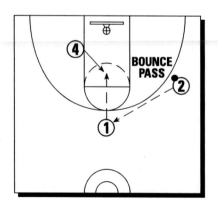

If we do *flash* our post into the middle of the zone, we feel the best time to do this is on the *reversal* of the ball.

SLIDING TO OPEN AREAS

DIAGRAM 16-7.

To make use of this concept of moving players around the zone into openings, we run what we call *tilt*. We start in a 1-2-2 set. The point guard brings the ball down on a *gap penetration* and makes a pass to 2.

DIAGRAM 16-8.

On the pass to 2, the weakside post, 5, flashes to the ballside high post. On the pass from 2 to 5, 4 automatically steps to the front of the rim. 2 moves to the baseline, 3 moves to the weakside baseline, and 1 slides away. 5 must catch the ball, look low, and then look opposite.

We like to screen the front, middle, and back of a zone. We prefer to *screen the front and back* of the zone more than the middle.

DIAGRAM 16-9.

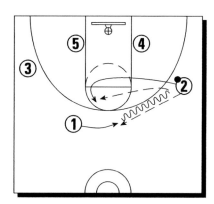

We use what we call *shallow* to screen the front of the zone. We once again set up in the 1-2-2 set. 1, the point guard, comes down and dribble-clears with either wing. Once the point guard replaces the wing, he looks inside and then passes out to 2.

DIAGRAM 16-10.

On the pass from 1 to 2, the offside wing, 3, must look to screen the guard. 2 makes two dribbles off the screen set by 3 and looks to shoot. At the same time, 5 moves to the corner, and 4 steps into the middle of the lane. This creates a 3-on-2 situation for the offense.

DIAGRAM 16-11.

In screening the *back of the zone*, we run what we call *counter*. This is keyed by a short corner pass which is usually caused by stretching the zone. 2 has driven toward the top of the key and the defense has followed him. Seeing the defensive forward go with 2, 4 steps into the short corner. 2 stops his dribble and passes back to 4.

DIAGRAM 16-12.

On this pass, 5, who had filled the high post on the ballside cuts to the basket. 5 would make this cut no matter where he was.

DIAGRAM 16-13.

4 returns the pass to 2, 2 passes to 1, 1 passes to 3 and 5 rolls back to the ball to post up on the block. 4 comes out of the short corner to screen the weakside defensive forward.

DIAGRAM 16-14.

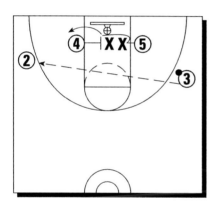

3, seeing 4 move in to screen, skip-passes to 2, who has moved to the baseline on the weakside.

DIAGRAM 16-15.

If the defensive forward tries to fight over 4's screen, 4 pivots in the direction that the defense is fighting and gives the impression of asking for the ball. You might say that this is an illegal screen, but we have as yet to be called for this.

DIAGRAM 16-16.

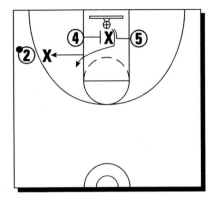

If the defensive forward gets around 4's screen, 4 moves into the lane and looks to screen the defensive center. Upon seeing this, 5 comes around 4's screen and looks for the ball.

DIAGRAM 16-17.

We also run what we call *opposite* to screen the back of the zone. As before, we set up in a 1-2-2 set. On the pass from 1 to 3, the ballside post moves across the zone and screens the weakside defensive forward. 4 cuts off the screen in front of the defensive center and asks for the ball. If the defensive center comes with 4, we go over the top of the zone to 5 for the lob. If the center doesn't come with 4, pass to 4 and run *tilt*.

These are some of the concepts and set plays we use in attacking zones. I hope you can take one or two ideas from these and incorporate them into what you run against a zone.

Before I close, I would like to share *two set plays* we run against man-to-man defense. We call these two "*4*" and "*4 Down.*" We start both in a 1-4 set.

DIAGRAM 16-18.

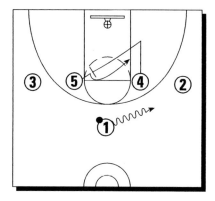

In "4," our point guard comes down and dribbles to one side or the other. As 1 makes his move, the post on the ballside, 4, slides down the lane and comes back up the middle of the lane to back-screen for the weakside post 5. Player 5 rolls down the lane off 4's backscreen and posts up on the block.

DIAGRAM 16-19.

After setting the backscreen, 4 steps out and 1 passes to 4. Player 2 runs a flex cut off 5. Player 1 slides to the wing, and 5 makes himself big. If 5 is open, 4 passes to 5.

DIAGRAM 16-20.

If 5 is not open, 4 passes to 1 and down-screens for 2, who we hit for a jump shot.

DIAGRAM 16-21.

On "*4 Down,*" after the pass from 1 to 4 and the flex cut by 2, 4 passes to 3 and 3 looks to dump the ball inside to 2. If 2 isn't open, he goes and sets a cross-screen for 5, and 4 moves down the lane to down-screen for 2. 3 looks to hit 5 for a dunk/power move or to 2 for a three-pointer. If nothing opens up off these two plays, we move into our motion.